34.60
10/11/11

Janis Joplin

"Take Another Little Piece of My Heart"

Read about other

American REBELS

James Dean
*"Dream As If You'll
Live Forever"*

0-7660-2537-3

Kurt Cobain
*"Oh Well, Whatever,
Nevermind"*

0-7660-2426-1

Jimi Hendrix
"Kiss The Sky"

0-7660-2449-0

Madonna
"Express Yourself"

0-7660-2442-3

Janis Joplin

"Take Another Little Piece of My Heart"

Edward Willett

 Enslow Publishers, Inc.
40 Industrial Road
Box 398
Berkeley Heights, NJ 07922
USA
http://www.enslow.com

To my big brother Jim, who, like Janis, was a Texas teenager in the '60s.

Library of Congress Cataloging-in-Publication Data

Willett, Edward, 1959-
  Janis Joplin: Take another little piece of my heart / by Edward Willett.
      p. cm.—(American rebels)
  Summary: "A biography of Janis Joplin. Presents a comprehensive look at her life and her music"—Provided by publisher.
  Includes bibliographical references (p.   ) and index.
  ISBN-13: 978-0-7660-2837-1
  ISBN-10:   0-7660-2837-2
  1. Joplin, Janis—Juvenile literature. 2. Singers—United States Biography—Juvenile literature. 3. Rock musicians—United States—Biography—Juvenile literature. I. Title.
  ML3930.J65W55 2008
  782.42166092—dc22
  [B]
                                                     2006039768
Printed in the United States of America

10 9 8 7 6 5 4 3 2 1

To Our Readers: We have done our best to make sure all Internet Addresses in this book were active and appropriate when we went to press. However, the author and the publisher have no control over and assume no liability for the material available on those Internet sites or on other Web sites they may link to. Any comments or suggestions can be sent by e-mail to comments@enslow.com or to the address on the back cover.

Cover Photo: ©Henry Diltz/The Image Works

Photo Credits: AP, pp. 6, 18, 24, 44, 72, 77, 86, 101, 105, 106, 109, 119, 128; Everett Collection, Inc., pp. 30, 92; Mrs. Marge Beaver, Photography Plus, NOAA Photo Library, p. 11; Photo by Peter Larsen/Rex Features, courtesy Everett Collection, p. 68.

Contents

Janis Joplin performing at an outdoor concert.

Introduction

On Saturday afternoon, June 17, 1967, a band with
the name of Big Brother and the Holding Company took
to the stage of the Monterey International Pop Festival
at the Monterey County Fairgrounds, eighty miles south
of San Francisco.

Big Brother's lead singer, a young woman named
Janis Joplin, was nervous. She had been singing with Big
Brother for a year, and so far the group hadn't made
much headway. They weren't a top draw even in San
Francisco, their hometown. Now here they were facing
their biggest audience yet. Forty thousand people had
turned out for the festival, but they were there to see
Otis Redding and British imports like The Who and Jimi
Hendrix. They weren't particularly interested in Big
Brother, which was why the band had been given a slot

on the program on Saturday afternoon, hardly prime time at a rock concert.

A documentary about the festival was being filmed by D. A. Pennebaker that weekend for ABC-TV, but the cameras weren't pointed at the stage when Big Brother and Janis Joplin launched into "Down on Me," "Road Block," and "Ball and Chain." Instead, they were pointed at the audience, where they captured the overwhelmed response of Mama Cass of the hit group the Mamas and the Papas.

> **"When I sing," Janis Joplin once said, "I feel, oh, I feel, well, like when you're first in love."**

When Big Brother finished its set, the audience exploded. The organizers were dumbfounded. Critics were ecstatic. Jazz critic Nat Hentoff wrote that Janis's performance left him limp and feeling that he'd been "in contact with an overwhelming life force." Greil Marcus, another critic, noted that Janis went so far out that he wondered how she ever managed to get back.[1]

"When I sing," Janis Joplin once said, "I feel, oh, I feel, well, like when you're first in love . . . I feel chills, weird feelings slipping all over my body, it's a supreme emotional and physical experience."[2]

At the Monterey Pop Festival, the audience felt the same way when they heard Janis Joplin perform. Brought back for an encore to ensure that this time their performance would be filmed, Janis and Big Brother wowed the audience again.

For Janis, it was vindication. Letting her feelings take hold, letting it "all hang out," had been something she'd always been counseled against, something that had led to taunts and ridicule in high school and beyond.

Before the Monterey Pop Festival, few people had heard of Janis Joplin. Afterward, almost everyone had. For the next three years, like a falling star, she would blaze a trail of outrageous behavior and incredible music across the pop-culture sky of 1960s America.

But then, like a falling star, her light would abruptly go out.

Chapter 1

Frilled Frocks and Bridge

The short but eventful life of Janis Joplin began in Port Arthur, Texas, located in southeast Texas just off the Gulf of Mexico and just west of the Louisiana border. It was founded and named by Kansas railway promoter Arthur E. Stilwell. Stilwell wanted to link Kansas City to the Gulf of Mexico by rail, because he had just launched the Kansas City, Pittsburgh, and Gulf Railroad. He and his backers acquired land on the western shore of Sabine Lake, a freshwater lake just inland from the Gulf and connected to it by a natural opening known as Sabine Pass.

Stillwell wanted the new city to be both a major tourist resort and an important seaport. He planned beautiful broad boulevards and avenues and grand homes along the lakeshore. A canal was cut along the western edge of the lake, connecting the site of the new town to deep water at Sabine Pass. Port Arthur was formally incorporated in 1898.[1]

Early in the twentieth century, Stillwell lost financial
control of the project to John W. Gates, a Wall Street
speculator whose nickname was Bet-a-Million. Gates
had made his fortune selling barbed wire across the
West. The company he formed eventually became
the giant corporation U.S. Steel.

Gates extended and deepened the canal so that ships
could sail it all the way to the cities of Beaumont and
Orange. Unfortunately, that cut off Port Arthur from the
lakeshore, ruining the view of the expensive lakeside

An aerial photo of Port Arthur, Texas, Janis's hometown.

homes and reducing Port Arthur's appeal as a tourist destination.

That appeal faded further as Port Arthur became inextricably linked to the burgeoning Texas oil industry. By the 1960s, the town buildings seemed almost lost among the huge oil refineries, storage tanks, and chemical plants. And because in those days natural gas was simply released into the air, the Golden Triangle region, encompassing the towns of Port Arthur, Orange, and Beaumont, smelled like rotting eggs. This smell from a nearby sulfur plant may have contained sulfur dioxide, a colorless, poisonous gas. In the air people breathe, the substance can irritate the eyes and respiratory system. It may also dissolve in water droplets to form acid rain, which can harm or even kill wildlife and damage buildings.

But oil also means money and good jobs, and it was the need for both that brought Janis's parents to Port Arthur before she was born.

The Flapper and the Bootlegger

Dorothy East and Seth Joplin met in Amarillo, Texas, on a blind date. Dorothy, the daughter of Cecil and Laura East, was known in Amarillo for her beautiful singing. She particularly liked Broadway show tunes, and in high school she won the lead role in a citywide stage production. The Broadway director the organizers brought in told Dorothy he could get her work in New York, but he recommended against it. She took his advice and, instead, applied to Texas Christian University in Fort Worth.

Disappointed that the university had only one voice teacher, who only taught opera, Dorothy returned to Amarillo after a single year and began helping at radio station KGNC. She was known as a free spirit, scandalizing her parents by adopting the flapper styles of short hair, close-fitting dresses,

> **[Dorothy] showed flashes of the same rebelliousness for which her daughter Janis would later be notorious.**

snazzy hats, and high heels. She also smoked and once accidentally swore on air. She showed flashes of the same rebelliousness for which her daughter Janis would later be notorious.

Seth Joplin was the son of Seeb, who ran the Amarillo stockyards, and Florence Joplin. At the time he met Dorothy East, Seth was taking a break from engineering studies at Texas A&M—studies he never finished. A lack of money forced him to give up his schooling one semester shy of a degree. A bit of a rebel himself, he made bathtub gin during the last days of Prohibition and smoked marijuana (which was legal then). While courting Dorothy, he took the only job he could find, as a gas-station attendant. Dorothy worked as a credit clerk in the local Ward's department store, eventually becoming head of the department.

In 1935, in the depths of the Depression, Seth got a break. His best friend from college recommended him for a job at the Texas Company (later Texaco) in Port Arthur. Dorothy quit her job to follow Seth, and she soon found work in the credit department at Sears. With two incomes, they were finally able to afford to marry, which they did on October 20, 1936.

Seth worked at the only Texaco plant that made containers for petroleum. When World War II broke out, his job was considered so vital that although he was called to join the armed forces three times, each time he was deferred.

Shortly after Seth and Dorothy married, Dorothy's parents' marriage broke up. Dorothy's mother, Laura, and her younger sister, Mimi, came to live with Seth and Dorothy. Needing more space, they bought their first house, a two-bedroom brick bungalow on the edge of town. For fun, Dorothy and Seth liked to cross the Sabine River and party in the bars in Vinton, Louisiana.

In mid-1942, Dorothy became pregnant. Janis Lyn Joplin was born at 9:30 A.M. on January 19, 1943.

Janis Joplin Makes Her Entrance

Although Janis was three weeks early and weighed only five and a half pounds, she thrived. After all, she had parents, a grandmother, and an aunt doting on her. When Janis was three, Laura and Mimi moved out to a place of their own.

As a child, Janis wasn't rebellious at all. In fact, Dorothy Joplin said later that Janis was easy to care for—not too docile, but not overactive, either—and cheerful by nature.

Dorothy, who believed a mother's place was at home, quit her job to look after Janis full-time. She made her beautiful dresses and blouses with ruffles, ribbons, and frills, and took her to the First Christian Church for church school, which Dorothy eventually taught.

Seth, who started work at 5:30 A.M., got to spend time with his daughter when he got home in the afternoon. Janis would wait for him on the front porch, he'd give her a hug, and they'd sit and talk.

As a child, Janis wasn't rebellious at all.

One day, Dorothy overheard her husband telling Janis about making bathtub gin in college. "'Is that the proper topic for a conversation with a child?' she asked him later," Laura Joplin, Janis's younger sister, wrote in her biography of Janis, *Love, Janis*. "Pop refused to argue the point; instead, he quit spending the evening time visiting with Janis on the front step. Janis was crushed and never knew why."[2]

Janis's mother introduced her daughter to music well before Janis started school. She bought an old upright piano and taught Janis how to play it. "She and Janis sat on the piano bench together, with Janis singing the simple nursery songs Dorothy taught her," Laura wrote. "Janis often lay in bed at night singing those songs, over and over, to put herself to sleep."[3]

But Janis's father found the noise of a child practicing scales annoying. Also, Dorothy had recently undergone an operation to remove her thyroid gland.

The operation destroyed her singing voice, although her speaking voice was fine. Seth Joplin thought having the piano around would be too emotionally painful for his wife, so the piano was sold, ending Janis's first flirtation with formal musical training.

In 1949, after two miscarriages, the Joplins had a second child, Laura Lee, and moved to a larger three-bedroom house at 3130 Lombardy Drive, in a neighborhood called Griffing Park. Four years later, in 1953, Janis's brother, Michael Ross, was born.

Janis was bright, friendly, and inquisitive. Laura wrote:

> People might have found her features plain if a buoyant spirit and zest for life hadn't overshadowed her looks. She was a child who

Janis Joplin: Her Own Tall Tale?

Dorothy Joplin said that Janis particularly loved magical, fantastical tales like J.R.R. Tolkien's books *The Hobbit* and *The Lord of the Rings*.

J. R. R. Tolkien (1892-1973), was an English author and scholar, who wrote a popular series of novels about an imaginary people called hobbits. Tolkien introduced the short, hairy-footed hobbits in *The Hobbit*. He continued their story in three related novels called *The Lord of the Rings*.

In *The Hobbit*, Bilbo Baggins, a hobbit, discovers a ring that conveys the power of invisibility but also corrupts the user. The hero of *The Lord of the Rings* is Frodo Baggins, Bilbo's cousin. After many adventures, Frodo destroys the ring so that Sauron, the evil Dark Lord, cannot use it.

liked people. She always made strangers welcome.
Her sensitivity to others showed in a considerate
willingness to go out of her way to include others
in play.[4]

Aside from singing herself to sleep and singing in
the church choir and, in junior high school, in the Glee
Club, Janis showed no particular aptitude for or interest
in music. She was much more interested in art. She
began to draw as soon as she could hold a pencil. Her
mother even arranged private art lessons for her when
she was in the third and fourth grades.

Janis also loved to read, a love that continued
throughout her life. She learned to read before she
entered school and had a library card even before that.

Janis even began writing her own plays in the first
grade and staging them with her friends as puppet
shows in a puppet theater her mother built for her in
the backyard.

A "Strikingly Timid Child"

Janis entered junior high with a good but unspectacular
academic record. Several of her childhood friends moved
out of town when she was in the sixth grade, and she
had to ride a bus to the junior high, which was farther
away than her grade school had been. She found the
rowdy kids on the bus frightening—she was a "strikingly
timid child," biographer Myra Friedman wrote—but
once she started traveling to junior high via a car pool
instead of on the bus, she adjusted quickly.

17

The limitations of Port Arthur meant that finding something interesting for the whole family to do took some imagination on the part of Janis's father. He hit upon taking them down to the post office to look at the Wanted posters. "It was a little unusual," he agreed later, "but it was somewhere to go. That wasn't the real reason, the Wanted Men. We'd just roam around the deserted building and read about all the people who were wanted for murders. We'd go any unusual place we could."[5]

Everyone who knew Janis when she was a child praised her when biographer Myra Friedman interviewed them not long after Janis's death. "Janis helped out in the library; Janis helped out at the church. Janis won an artwork contest for the cover of a junior high

A young Janis Joplin smiles for the camera.

publication; Janis did posters for the library. Janis was cooperative; Janis was shy. Janis was 'just like everybody else,'" she wrote.[6]

But in junior high, as Janis approached adolescence, signs began to appear that perhaps Janis wasn't "just like everybody else" after all. Her teachers began to give her unsatisfactory marks in work habits and citizenship. She was also, according to her friends, naive and gullible, someone who could be led to believe all kinds of preposterous stories and who was always eager to please other people.

Janis did all the things expected of a proper young girl in Port Arthur in the 1950s. She joined the Junior Reading Circle for Culture, the Tri Hi Y club, and the Glee Club, which gave Janis her first public singing opportunity outside of church—she sang a solo in the Christmas pageant. As bridge was a passion of her parents, Janis even took bridge lessons. In fact, she met her first boyfriend, Jack Smith, when they played bridge together in the seventh grade in the Ladies Aid Society's Bridge for Cultural Improvement club.

Despite occasional problems with talking too much in class or doodling when she should have been taking notes, Janis seemed destined to sail smoothly into Port Arthur society, following the course prescribed for young ladies: high school, university, marriage, house, kids.

But in high school, smooth sailing gave way to stormy waters.

Chapter 2

The Rebellion Begins

Janis Joplin would later recall her childhood years as being nearly idyllic. "Then the whole world turned!" she said. "It just turned on me!"[1]

That "turning" happened at Thomas Jefferson High School, but maybe it began even earlier, as Janis began to look beyond the immediate concerns of childhood at the larger world around her.

"Probably about the ninth grade," Janis's friend Karleen Bennett said, "she started having opinions of her own. A question about integration came up and all Janis said was she thought integration was fine. You just didn't do that in Port Arthur."[2]

Integration—allowing blacks and whites to mix freely, attend the same schools, ride the same buses, and, in general, ensuring both races enjoyed the same rights and privileges—was beginning to be a hot issue in the United States in the late 1950s. The Supreme Court had banned school segregation in 1954, when Janis was in seventh grade, but integration hadn't yet come to Port Arthur.

A Segregated Society

In Port Arthur, the black minority lived its own segregated life in the oldest part of town, an area downtown bordered by Houston Avenue, where there were lots of black clubs and a lively nightlife that white kids were forbidden to visit. Professional offices had segregated waiting rooms, the hospital had a separate wing for black patients, and water fountains bore signs that said Whites Only.

Janis found out the hard way about segregation and intolerance. For simply saying she didn't see anything wrong with integration, she was taunted for the rest of the school year.

Racial segregation wasn't the only kind of segregation in Port Arthur. The Joplins were part of the "proper," church-going, white middle-class society of the city. But there was another side to Port Arthur. Port cities like Port Arthur are frequented by sailors, and sailors are not known for spending their time on shore sipping coffee and playing bridge.

It wasn't talked about, but everybody knew about it—including the teenagers. And that darker, seedier side of the city included prostitution and gambling attracted some of them, especially those who, like Janis, were beginning to find out that they didn't really fit the mold that Port Arthur's polite society did its best to pour them into.

Laura Joplin remembered how disillusioned Janis was when, while she was working as a salesclerk in a toy store, her boss told her to mark up the price on toys one day, then mark them back down to their original price the next day—but put up a sale sign. Janis told her mother it was dishonest

"Janis did the only thing a bright, determined, idealistic girl could do," Laura wrote. "She went searching. She simply turned her head away from the prescribed path to face the layers of life that society had told her were not the proper ones for a young lady. . . . [S]he decided that if the good people weren't all good, then perhaps the supposedly bad people weren't all bad. She was off to see for herself."[3]

Janis's looks also contributed to her growing sense of alienation as she entered high school. When she started tenth grade, she was still slim—too slim, with slender hips and a flat chest. Having skipped a grade, she was as much as a year and a half younger than her classmates, and she became self-conscious about her lack of physical development.

But as time went on, she lost her slimness and became overweight. Not only that, she developed severe acne. At the time, people thought bad skin in adolescence was caused by eating fatty or sugary foods or not washing your face enough. A dermatologist tried several treatments, even freezing some of the biggest pimples with dry ice, but to no effect.

The result? "She'd been cute and all of a sudden she was ugly," was how one classmate put it. Janis's high-school friend Grant Lyons said that "once you turned fourteen in Port Arthur, Texas, you were in a kind of sexual race if you were a girl. And if you didn't have the goods, well, then, you fell behind. The girls who were popular were good-looking, and Janis wasn't."[4]

Janis was "different" in another way, too: She read and she was smart.

Another high-school classmate, Kristen Bowen, said, "The main goal of high school was to not be different." But, wrote Janis's sister, Laura, "Janis looked around school and saw the hierarchy of social groups. At the top were those in class government; next came the athletes, the cheerleaders, the kids with great personalities whom everyone liked, and finally a giant mess of others of indistinguishable quality. She clearly felt among the last group, while her ego felt she deserved to be in the top tier."[5]

And so, Janis began to explore alternatives.

The Little Theater Gang

Her alternative interests began to reveal themselves even before she entered high school. Between the ninth and tenth grades, Janis joined the summer program of the Port Arthur Little Theater, painting scenery and ushering. (She played only one role, in a production of *Sunday Costs Five Pesos*.)

A 1970 photo of Janis Joplin

Grant Lyons's mother ran the Little Theater program. "Grant hung out with a group of intellectuals who were united by their disdain for the level of mental sophistication of their classmates and the town in general," wrote Laura Joplin. The group consisted mainly of Grant's friends: Dave Moriaty, Adrian Haston, Jim Langdon, and Randy Tennant. That summer, Janis discovered, as Laura puts it, that within the Little Theater group, "adolescent cynicism was their modus operandi," and they took "great delight in mocking anyone brazen enough to admit they believed in anything good."[6]

In their discussions (their socializing consisted mainly of driving a car to some out-of-the-way spot, sitting and talking), they even questioned the existence of God. "Janis realized that the groovy people didn't even believe in God, the Ten Commandments, and hell," Laura wrote. "Discovering the hypocrisy of society and the possibility that God wasn't guiding things after all freed her from adopting the status quo. . . . Perhaps the supposedly 'bad' wasn't so at all, especially if the protectors of local social codes were breaking them whenever they could get away with it."[7]

The group of five boys and Janis would eventually form a tight-knit group, although, at first, the boys weren't sure what to make of the girl insinuating herself into their close group. Over time, they came to accept her, not so much as a girl but as "one of the boys."

The Beats

Every culture has its counterculture, and in the 1950s, the counterculture to the kind of straitlaced world Janis and the boys were struggling against was called Beat culture.

The name came from a group of writers known as the Beats, the best known of whom were Jack Kerouac, Allen Ginsberg, and William S. Burroughs. All three met in the 1940s and shared an apartment in New York City. They used to hang out in cafeterias in Times Square, talking about ideas while taking advantage of free coffee refills. When Herbert Huncke joined the group, he brought with him the word *beat*, which was slang used by jazz players for being totally spent and worn-out. Later, a San Francisco columnist coined the term *beatnik*, based on the name of the first satellite to orbit Earth, the Soviet Union's *Sputnik*, but the term was not intended as a compliment.

The Beats saw themselves as outlaws in what had become, after World War II, a very conservative culture. They listened to jazz, they smoked marijuana, they took speed, and they wrote poetry and stories that were unlike anything else being written at the time. The most famous Beat poem is Allen Ginsburg's *Howl*, a book-length poem that's about the adventures of his Beat companions. The most famous Beat book is undoubtedly Jack Kerouac's *On the Road*.

The Beats embraced causes that were out of the mainstream (for the time), such as pacifism, ecology, and economic reform. Ann Charters, who edited a collection of Beat writings called *The Portable Beat Reader*, said in an interview that "I think of the values they were looking for as moral values—a reaction against capitalism, materialism, Mammon, that Ginsburg talks about in the poem, *Howl* . . . I find that everywhere. There's no question about it, they were counter-culture and they also were counter-culture not just to be different, but because they thought there were serious problems with capitalist America."[8]

By the time Janis was in high school, the Beats were well known and they were much talked about symbols of rebellion against the prevailing culture, so it wasn't surprising that the group of Little Theater rebels admired the Beats. They were, in fact, the closest thing Port Arthur had to beatniks.

Guides for a Generation

When Allen Ginsburg's famous poem *Howl* was published in 1957, the publisher was charged with publishing an obscene book, and copies of the book were seized by San Francisco customs officers. But the poem sold more than a million copies, and it signaled the beginning of a new openness in the culture.

On the Road, based on Jack Kerouac's travels across the country in the late 1940s, inspired a whole generation with the idea of leaving home and setting out with no particular plans or destination, just to see what was out there and maybe "find themselves."

Early Rebellions

Even so, Janis wasn't fully committed to that particular form of rebellion early in her high-school career, and the Port Arthur beatniks weren't committed to her, either. Women didn't really have a place in Beat culture, not as intellectual equals, anyway. Janis probably wasn't even fully accepted by the group until her sophomore year.

According to Laura Joplin, Janis actually hung out with an entirely different group of rebels, the guys who were into cars, wore their hair slicked back (like Fonzie in the old TV show *Happy Days*), and liked to wear black leather jackets with the name of their car clubs stitched on the back. Janis dyed her hair orange for a while like the other girls in the car club, and she dated one of the car-club guys, Rooney Paul.

For the first couple of years of high school, she continued to do well academically.

But when she was with Jack Smith, the boy she met in the bridge club who wasn't part of either the beatniks or the car-club guys, she wouldn't allow him to curse and joke with her the way they did.

Janis continued to be interested in art, though her subject matter made her parents uncomfortable: She loved painting nudes. Once she painted a nude figure on the inside panel of her bedroom closet door, but her parents made her paint over it. And at least for the first couple of years of high school, she continued to do well academically, earning A's and B's and a few C's. Her teachers complimented her scholastic ability while warning that she exhibited poor behavior in class—like talking too much, for instance.

Leaving the Mainstream

But as high school continued, Janis became more and more a part of the beatniks and less and less integrated into the mainstream of high-school life. She and her friends read "weird" stuff—especially the Beats, but other things, too, from Irving Stone's fictionalized biography of Vincent van Gogh, *Lust for Life*, to D. H. Lawrence's *Lady Chatterley's Lover* (banned as obscene by the U.S. postmaster general) to the hard-boiled detective novels of Mickey Spillane.

They began to dress differently, too. Janis's mother kept trying to help Janis fit in by making or buying her nice clothes, but Janis usually refused to wear them. Forbidden by school rules to wear pants, she wore instead black or purple leotards and skirts that ended just above the knee, when most other girls were wearing skirts with hems just below the knee.

And then there was the music. "Music wasn't just background noise," wrote Alice Echols in her biography of Janis Joplin, *Scars of Sweet Paradise*. "It was a declaration of difference." The music they sought out was "renegade music, untainted by commercialism." The rock 'n' roll of the late fifties and early sixties was too commercial, too smooth, too mass-produced. "It seemed so shallow, all oop-boop," Janis said later. "It had *nothing*."[9]

The gang used to cram into Jim Langdon's bedroom to listen to his portable hi-fi. Grant Lyons liked serious folk music, "roots music." Jim, Adrian, and Dave loved the jazz of Dave Brubeck and other artists, and Dave and Jim had large collections of classical music, too. Janis discovered she loved old-time black blues singers when Grant brought a recording by Leadbelly.

Another singer Janis loved was Odetta, one of the younger black folk musicians. One night, while the gang was riding around, they were all singing along with an Odetta tune—all except Janis, who refused to join in. Finally, unable to bear the way they were butchering the tune, she burst into song—and shocked the boys into silence. "She just burst out and sounded exactly like Odetta," Dave Moriaty remembered. "That showed us up. We used to sing folk songs on our way driving anywhere. Well, after that, we still did, but it wasn't the same. We weren't all in the same class anymore."[10] It was one of the earliest hints of the music that was to come.

A photo of Huddie "Leadbelly" Ledbetter performing.

The gang's nighttime cruises often took them into Louisiana, where bars served hard liquor (they only served beer and wine in Port Arthur), and where minors were often served alcohol. There they heard even more music.

Who Was Leadbelly?

Huddie Ledbetter, better known as Leadbelly, was a black blues singer from Louisiana-just across the state line from Port Arthur. Leadbelly, an ex-con, was discovered by a musicologist collecting songs from southern prisons.

Although Leadbelly died in 1949, his music lived on, and it helped spark renewed interest in folk music in the 1950s and 1960s.

Taunts and Insults

As Janis withdrew from the mainstream, she began to draw taunts and insults from the "normal" kids. While her beatnik friends were still in school, they served as a kind of buffer, but most of them were a year older than she was. So, in her senior year in high school, she had less support and fewer friends, although by that time a few other younger boys had gravitated to the beatniks, including Jack Smith, Tary Owens, and Philip Carter. And whereas the boys had always had other activities that made them more acceptable to the general high-school student population—Grant Lyons was a football star, Jim Langdon was a prize-winning trombone player, and Dave Moriaty edited the high-school paper—Janis had pretty much alienated everyone.

Janis spent a lot of time at Karleen's house; Karleen's parents liked her. She also began spending as much time as possible at the Sage, Port Arthur's first coffeehouse. On New Year's Eve 1959, the beatniks held a party at the Sage, and Janis sang.

An incident shortly afterward seems to have made her schoolmates despise her even more. On January 26, 1960, just before her seventeenth birthday, Janis talked Jim Langdon and two other boys at the Sage, Clyde Wade and Dale Gauthier, into going to New Orleans to listen to music. She borrowed her father's car and lied to her parents, saying she was spending the night at Karleen's. She expected to return the next morning and that her parents would never find out. But on the way back, with Clyde driving, they had a minor accident that wrecked the radiator and stalled the car.

When the police showed up, they threatened the boys with charges under the Mann Act, which makes it a federal crime to transport individuals under the age of eighteen across state lines to engage in sexual activity. The boys were over eighteen, but Janis wasn't.

In the end, no one was charged. But Janis already had a reputation for being sexually promiscuous (although she almost certainly wasn't), and the New Orleans escapade sealed it. Faced with gossip and innuendo, Janis fought back by doing her best to live up to her new reputation.

> **"She picked up the banner of social outcast and began taunting them with it."**
>
> **—Laura Joplin**

"Before this incident, Janis had only seemed a bit kooky to other kids because she wore beatnik clothes," Laura wrote. "After the gossip about the New Orleans trip in her last semester in high school, she picked up the banner of social outcast and began taunting them with it."[11]

The school counselor called Janis in; she later claimed she'd had a bottle of wine hidden in her purse all the time he talked to her. She fought with her parents, especially her mother. Her parents sent her to another counselor to try to help her deal with her anger at society. They considered family therapy. Her friends tried to help her by including her in parties, but even at a party, she felt excluded.

Janis herself later said of Port Arthur, "What's happening never happens there. It's all drive-in movies and Coke stands on the corner, and anyone with ambitions like me leaves as soon as they can or they're taken over, repressed, and put down. . . . All I was looking for was some kind of personal freedom, and other people who felt the same way."[12]

In May of 1960, Janis graduated from Thomas Jefferson High School. In the fall, she'd be heading to college. Things would have to be better there.

Wouldn't they?

Chapter 3

From College to the Coast

Following most other college-bound students from Port Arthur, Janis enrolled in Lamar State College of Technology in nearby Beaumont the fall after she graduated. She hoped to meet new people with different viewpoints, people who could appreciate the things she thought were important.

Unfortunately, Lamar wasn't the best school at which to find those people. "You take all those high schools (in the Golden Triangle), roll a lasso around them, pull it tight and you have Lamar Tech," Grant Lyons said. He'd received a football scholarship to Tulane, so he didn't end up at Lamar. Of the old beatnik group in Port Arthur, Jim Langdon, Adrian Haston, and Tary Owens did.[1]

And things were at least a *little* better at Lamar because the intellectual rebels from "all those high schools" could now band together and form a slightly larger group—still a minority, but not quite as isolated.

They gravitated to their own area of the student union and pretty much kept to themselves.

But the gossip about Janis that had plagued her in Port Arthur followed her to Lamar—not surprising, since so many of her high-school classmates ended up there. Janis listed her major as art. Her sister, Laura, wrote that she worked hard at it, at least at first, but Janis's college friends dispute that. Instead, she seems to have really majored in "hanging out." She and a new friend, Patti Skaff, would go to bars in Beaumont when they were supposed to be in class. "We'd just drink and talk and drink and talk. Who knows what we talked about," Patti remembered.[2]

Drinking and talking, talking and drinking, that was what Janis and all of her friends did. Several of the boys had off-campus apartments where they could party, and since some were old enough to buy liquor legally, there was plenty of it. Janis, who had to sneak out of her dorm after the curfew check, sometimes came back so drunk that her friends had to lift her up from the lawn and over the balcony railing on the second floor, where her friends inside the dorm would pull her in.

Even if Laura is right and Janis did work at her art to begin with, it didn't last. She met a new student, Tommy Stopher, who she thought was a much better painter. Janis gave up on the idea of being an artist.

A Growing Interest

By the end of her first semester, Janis couldn't see the point of Lamar any longer. It certainly wasn't providing her the intellectual stimulation she wanted, even if it was providing her with plenty of opportunities to party. Her parents weren't pleased.

Mrs. Joplin was working at a business college at the time, so at her urging Janis enrolled in Port Arthur College in a short-term training program, studying clerical skills like keypunch and typing. She attended classes half days for four months, and in that time missed all or a portion of nineteen days because she claimed she was ill. Obviously her heart wasn't in it, but at least she picked up employable skills.

She spent a lot of her nonclass time with Patti, her friend from Lamar. They spent hours listening to music in a downtown record store. Sometimes, Janis would sing into a tape recorder belonging to Patti's father and then listen to herself. She didn't like what she heard.

Janis had given up on art, but her interest in music was growing, and her interest in singing—which she hadn't really done much of since her younger days singing in the church choir—may have been rekindled by seeing a friend from Lamar Tech, Frances Vincent, perform in the Beaumont Community Players' production of the musical *The Boy Friend*.

But Janis still didn't spend much time singing. She spent a lot more at wild, drunken parties with her friends.

Off to the Coast

Despite missing so many classes, Janis passed her secretarial exam in the summer of 1961. She and her

parents agreed that she should move to Los Angeles.
Seth and Dorothy Joplin hoped that removing Janis
from the local gang she hung out and partied with
might settle her down. Dorothy's two sisters, Barbara
and Mimi, lived in Los Angeles, and the Joplins hoped
they might provide a certain amount of supervision.

At first, Janis lived in an "artist's shack" out back of
her aunt Mimi's house in Brentwood. Mimi's husband,
Harry, painted there and kept a supply of oil paints and
canvases. Her first night, Janis stayed up half the night,
once again painting. She seemed to be off to a good start.

She also got a job, with the help of her aunts, as a
keypunch operator at the telephone company. Once she
had her own paycheck, she moved into an apartment
that her aunt Barbara helped her find. But Janis couldn't
afford the rent, and she soon moved in with Barbara and
her teenaged daughter, Jean. Janis and Barbara got along
very well, but Jean resented Janis's presence.

So Janis moved out again, to Venice Beach. Made
famous in a book by Lawrence Lipton called *The Holy
Barbarians*, Venice Beach had once been home to a
thriving, if poor, community of beatniks. But by the time
Janis got there, tourism had driven most of them off.
"The area had become mean-spirited," Laura Joplin
wrote. "Crime was commonplace—murders, robbery,
and rape. The amusement park stood rotting. At night
the beach belonged to the muggers. No longer on the
fringe of the drug world, it was now one of the centers.

Grass, Benzedrine, heroin, and codeine cough syrup all had their followings."

The real home of the Beats was supposed to be North Beach in San Francisco, and after a while Janis decided to check it out. She hitchhiked from Los Angeles to San Francisco, refusing her aunts' offer to buy her a bus ticket, and she stayed in San Francisco a couple of months. She bought a World War II bomber jacket, which she wore inside out so the sheepskin lining showed.

Partying With the Old Gang

She wore it when she returned to Port Arthur for Christmas, 1961. She also brought with her the same loud, over-the-top personality she'd developed throughout high school—only now it was even louder and cruder. Powell St. John, who would later be a close friend of Janis's, met her for the first time shortly after she returned from California, and he found her intimidating. He said until he met Janis, he'd never even seen a beatnik.

> **"We were creative, we were rebels, and we just didn't go for it."**
> **—Patti Skaff**

Over the next few months, she partied with her old gang. "We were creative, we were rebels, and we just didn't go for it," Patti Skaff said of all the trouble they got into, from car crashes to bar fights in Louisiana to minor run-ins with the police. "So we'd go out and do crazy things. We'd drive around and drive around in whoever's parents' car had any gas in it that we could get a hold of. We were just these people who wouldn't give up. And I guess we were on the verge of being put in jail or institutionalized."[3]

At one party, fueled by alcohol, Janis and Patti kissed each other on the mouth. Patti's husband, Dave McQueen, and Jim Langdon had just walked in. Nobody said anything, but much later, Dave lost his temper and threw his beer bottle at Patti, who was asleep between two men. The bottle missed Patti and instead hit Jack Smith.

Janis and Patti's relationship never developed into a homosexual one, but at another party Janis did have sex with a woman, probably for the first time.

The Music Begins

Partying, with lots of alcohol and lots of sex, seemed to be all Janis had in her life that winter in Texas, but something else began that would ultimately prove more important: She began to sing in public.

Not that her attempts were very successful. On New Year's Eve, right after her return from Venice, Janis performed at a Beaumont club. The gig had been arranged by Jim Langdon. Janis was supposed to sing a few songs with a jazz band led by Jim's friend Jimmy Simmons, but she was cut off after only one number. Her powerful, raucous voice just wasn't what they expected or wanted.

But Janis kept trying. Sometimes late at night, at clubs where a group Jim was in was playing, Janis would come up on stage to sing. She also sang at the Half-Way

House in Beaumont and The Purple Onion in Houston. And sometime in those early months of 1962, Janis Joplin recorded her first song—a jingle for a commercial for a bank in Nacogdoches, Texas. One of the groups Jim Langdon worked with, called Ray Solis, had signed to provide the music. Alas, the jingle was never used.

And then, one wild weekend, everything changed again: On a night when everyone else at a party headed off to the Louisiana bars as usual, Janis and Jack Smith instead ran off to Austin in Seth Joplin's car.

Janis Moves to Austin

Jack knew just where to go: 2812 ½ Nueces Street, an apartment house called the Ghetto. When they went in, at 5:37 A.M., they discovered a local folk musician sitting on top of the refrigerator playing the banjo.

The next day, she had to face the music back in Port Arthur for having driven off in her father's car without permission. Janis argued with her parents about what she planned to do with her life. In the end, Janis agreed to enroll in the University of Texas in Austin.

Janis wanted to live at the Ghetto, but there was no way her mother would agree to that. Nor would the university, which required freshman and sophomore girls to live in supervised housing. But she hung around the Ghetto. One place she didn't hang around was class. She enrolled as an art major, but took only one art class. She earned C's in anthropology and psychology and withdrew from five other courses.

The crowd she met at the Ghetto was the core

of the university's offbeat (and Beat) crowd. Among
mainstream students, the women wore bubble hairdos
and the men wore black suede loafers. Janis and her
friends wore men's white dress shirts with the tails
hanging out and blue jeans. Or they'd wear a black
turtleneck and black slacks with boots and sandals.
Janis liked to wear her World War II bomber jacket
(inside out, of course); she'd torn the sleeves off to make
it less hot. She let her hair grow long and hang loose,
and she didn't wear makeup.

The Ghetto group included musicians, writers,
cartoonists, and even spelunkers (cave explorers). They
were known for their outrageous behavior and wild
parties. They shot holes in walls, put fists through
windows, threw people into a fountain, and covered
walls with vulgar graffiti.

Music Matters

But just as important as rebellion was music. The
alternative music of the day was folk music, and in
the Ghetto, they were interested in hard-core folk
music: ethnic folk music, a term that in the early 1960s
covered acoustic blues and country, or "hillbilly" music.
And it was in Austin that Janis began to sing seriously
and to study and master the music that intrigued her.

In fact, she sang the night after she arrived in
Austin, accompanied by Powell St. John on harmonica
and Lanny Wiggins on bass. Janis eventually added the
Autoharp to the mix. They called themselves the Waller
Creek Boys (St. John and Wiggins were already The

It was in Austin that Janis began to sing seriously and to study and master the music that intrigued her.

Waller Creek Boys and didn't want to change the name). Later, they were "the Waller Creek Boys, featuring Janis Joplin."

Thursday nights the group often performed at the regular school-sponsored hootenanny (folk music night) at the student union. Musicians sat in a circle on the floor, sharing instruments and jumping in whenever there was a pause. Some of the performances were awful—but not the Waller Creek Boys, and especially not when Janis sang.

But the most important place they played in was a bar called Threadgill's.

Threadgill's

Threadgill's, run by Kenneth Threadgill, had begun life as a gas station. Threadgill's normally catered to rural people and truck drivers, but on Wednesday nights university students interested in folk music began to come out because most Wednesday nights Threadgill had bluegrass musicians perform. Each group received two dollars per night and all the beer they could drink.

Threadgill recognized Janis's talent and took a fatherly interest in her. Eddie Wilson, a later owner of Threadgill's, said, "He [Threadgill] was the only authority figure that Janis Joplin ever really seemed to respect. She was pretty rebellious, and Kenneth was just as sweet as he could be and tried to encourage her."[4]

Threadgill's wife liked her, too, and would sometimes try to brush her shaggy hair. So Janis sang a lot, and in the process, learned her music and her craft. Most importantly, wrote her sister, Laura, she learned to make an emotional connection to her music, by broadening her interest from folk to the much more emotionally charged blues.

The other important lesson Janis learned in Austin was that notoriety could help you succeed artistically. Among the Ghetto group were members of the staff of the *Texas Ranger*, a campus humor magazine. Its biting satire and an argument with the university administration over a poem the writers thought was funny and the administration thought was obscene had boosted its circulation from five thousand to twenty-five thousand.

For a while, Janis's boyfriend, Bill Killeen, was one of the *Texas Ranger's* editors. (He was her second serious boyfriend in Austin; the first was Powell St. John.) Her rooming house didn't allow male visitors, but Killeen had access to a vacant rental house belonging to a friend's father. Killeen and Janis lived there together in September and October. The relationship ended as much because they had to leave the house as because of any falling out.[5]

Sex, Drugs, and Folk Music

The phrase "sex, drugs, and rock 'n' roll" may not have yet been coined in 1962, but that was the lifestyle Janis was already living (except for the "rock 'n' roll" part,

Janis performing in December, 1969.

since she was still singing folk). She had sex with a lot
of men and a few women; the group included several
women who were, or at least thought to be, homosexual.
And like the rest of the group, she did drugs: peyote
(legal and cheap, but Janis reportedly didn't like it or
other hallucinogens, like LSD, much); marijuana (illegal
even to possess, which made it enjoyable to Janis); and
speed (amphetamines), which was actually handed out
by college health services during midterms and finals.[6]
But Janis's drug of choice, like the rest of the group, was
alcohol, primarily beer.

Shy and *retiring* were two words nobody ever applied
to Janis Joplin, then, or for the rest of her life. She could
be rude, abrasive, and downright mean. Whether it was
because she injured the pride of a fraternity boy one
night in a bar or because the Ghetto crowd saw it as

a joke, Janis was nominated for the Ugliest Man on Campus contest (she may even have nominated herself). The fact that she actually got votes, though, seems to have upset her—and may have contributed to her decision, shortly thereafter, to leave for San Francisco.

One thing that definitely contributed to her decision was a visit by former University of Texas student Chet Helms, just passing through on his way back to California. He liked the folk music he heard in Austin. He told Janis she would be a hit in San Francisco.

Janis believed him and decided to go. She could never make a career as a singer in Austin. Maybe she could in San Francisco, specifically North Beach. It was in North Beach where Allen Ginsberg had read his poem *Howl* on October 13, 1955. It was in North Beach where Lawrence Ferlinghetti, proprietor of the City Lights Pocket Book Shop, was arrested (and made nationally famous, along with his bookshop and North Beach) for publishing "obscene" material, when he attempted to bring copies of *Howl* into the country from Britain. North Beach was the West Coast heart of the Beat scene.

And so shortly after midnight one day in mid-January of 1963, after Janis sang one more time at Threadgill's, she and Chet Helms hit the road.

North Beach Bound

Their first stop was in Fort Worth, where Chet Helms's parents lived. Helms's parents weren't impressed with the wild, foulmouthed girl he had brought home. They fed Chet and Janis dinner, but wouldn't let them stay overnight. So the pair headed back out to the highway and continued hitchhiking, arriving in San Francisco a little over two days later.

North Beach contained the same kinds of people Janis had hung out with in Austin and Port Arthur. That very first night she sang at a shop called Coffee and Confusion on Upper Grant Avenue, and she received fourteen dollars from the appreciative audience.

Over the next few months, Janis lived hand to mouth, crashing in various apartments, holding down a few jobs (just enough to pick up unemployment insurance), and singing at a place called The Coffee Gallery, or occasionally at Coffee and Confusion, and bringing in a few dollars by passing the hat. She shoplifted (she was arrested in Berkeley for shoplifting her second month in California), and she panhandled.

She also drank. "Janis's tolerance for alcohol had reached a level where she could drink a lot with little visible effect," Laura Joplin wrote. "In fact, at only twenty years of age she was beginning to be compulsive about her liquid friend."[7]

Alcohol wasn't her only drug. The use of speed was common in the Beat scene, and Janis (who may well have tried it already during her earlier time in California) took to it readily.

But Janis also began meeting people who would be important to her for the rest of her life. James Gurley and Sam Andrew, future members of Janis's band Big

Brother and the Holding Company, sometimes played at
The Coffee Gallery. Other future musical stars Janis met
there included Marty Balin, later of the Jefferson
Airplane, and David Crosby, later of Crosby, Stills,
and Nash.

It was also at The Coffee Gallery that she met Linda
Gottfried, her longtime friend. At the time, Janis was
living for free in a basement on Sacramento Street,
courtesy of some folksingers who liked her singing. She

Janis in a Coffeehouse

In his 1997 book *Laid Bare: A Memoir of Wrecked
Lives and the Hollywood Death Trip*, author and
journalist John Gilmore described seeing Janis Joplin
perform in a San Francisco coffeehouse:

> She closed her eyes . . . and sang a blues number
> I'd heard in New Orleans the year before . . . she
> was good. She sang low, slurring almost as though
> choking back cries, underplaying words in a
> trembling way that carried the threat of something
> bottled up and moving inside her like a riptide.
> She coddled syllables with her mouth, did things
> to the words with her throat and tongue that gave
> them new meanings, that made you feel them
> more intensely, although there was a sense, too,
> that she wasn't even sure what she was doing. Her
> voice would crack a little—a sharp tone pushing
> through a soft word. It was odd, like she'd been
> struck with a pain, but she kept right on singing
> without slowing down, just pushing the words
> together.[8]

and Janis got on well together from the beginning, and Gottfried moved in with her.

Passionate About Her Music

Despite the daily struggle to find food to eat, Janis was passionate about her music.

In 1963, Janis appeared on a local radio show with Peter Albin, another future member of Big Brother and the Holding Company. Albin's brother had arranged for Janis and musicians Roger Perkins, Larry Hanks, and Billy Roberts, who had been performing together around town, to play at the upcoming San Francisco State Music Festival, but they never showed up.

It may have been because Janis had hurt her leg while trying to get on her Vespa motorcycle when drunk. Or it may have been that she decided on a whim to make her way to New York for a quick look at the East Coast version of the Beat scene, in Greenwich Village.

Whether she went to New York in 1963 or not, by the summer of 1964 she'd made up her mind to not just visit but to move there.

Chapter 4

New York to L.A.

Janis never intended to stay in New York permanently.
According to Linda Gottfried, Janis went to earn and
save some money without sullying her reputation as an
artist in San Francisco by actually working in California.[1]

Janis sang in New York, but not very much. She
probably told her mother she was singing more than
she really was: Dorothy Joplin sent her stage clothes—a
black blouse embroidered in bright orange and covered
with tiny mirrors and a red-and-white robe. Janis
wouldn't wear them: She said they were "too flashy."
That seems ironic, considering the flamboyant way she
dressed just a few years later, but in New York that year
she only wore black, with a large gold watch hanging
around her neck on a gold chain.

After four months in New York, Janis headed back to
San Francisco. She'd scraped together enough money
to buy a yellow Morris Minor convertible (it looked a
bit like a Volkswagen Beetle). She drove hundreds of

What is Methamphetamine?

Methamphetamine is a powerful drug nicknamed "speed." It quickly produces feelings of euphoria, strength, and alertness. Its misuse can be dangerous. Users may become mentally dependent on the drug if, when they go without it, they find the world a cold harsh place. Sudden withdrawal may cause depression, fatigue, or severe mental illness.

miles out of her way to visit her family in Port Arthur, surprising her sister, Laura, then in ninth grade, at summer band practice. She even gave Laura her old six-string guitar as she had bought a new twelve-string one.

On her way back to California, Janis stopped in Austin to see the old gang. By September of 1964 she was back in San Francisco. Before long, she was again sharing a place with Linda Gottfried and performing at local clubs.

In It For The Good Time

Janis was singing regularly, but you couldn't really call it a singing career.

Seth Joplin took Janis and Linda Gottfried to dinner, and according to Gottfried, he told them about the "Saturday Night Swindle, about how you hear over and over that if you work real hard you'll go out Saturday night and have a really good time. And everybody lives for that good time, but it never really happens." He wasn't judgmental about the way they lived, Gottfried said. "He just wanted to make sure Janis knew how to get around in the real world. He understood her." He urged the two to buy *Time* magazine every week and read it cover to cover to stay in touch with the "real world" and make independent decisions.[2]

Janis, though, said later that during that time she wasn't serious about anything. She was just in it for the good time. "She consumed alcohol flamboyantly," her sister wrote. "With the artistic community, she sampled other drugs for their potential to enhance the unbridled freedom she sought."[3]

Toward the end of 1964, Janis and Linda Gottfried realized they were addicted to speed. "I remember when we knew," Gottfried said. "We had planned to go to the de Young Muscum and then the Laundromat. On the way we looked at each other and said, 'Let's go home and do some meth.'" She added, "No one knew about drugs then. They were an experiment. We thought we were growing by leaps and bounds. We worked day and night. We did more paintings, more poems, and more songs."[4]

Like many speed addicts, Janis soon went from using it to dealing it a little. Then, in 1965, she began using heroin.

Janis also had a number of sexual relationships, with both men and women, usually very short-lived. She claimed she wasn't homosexual.

When she did pick a boyfriend, his name was Peter de Blanc whom Janis met in early 1965.

Janis's Fiancé

Laura Joplin described him as rich, intelligent, gentle, charismatic, and a meth enthusiast.

He seemed too good to be true, and he was. He lied about his past, telling all sorts of fanciful stories about what he had done. But Janis seems to have really loved him—and to have followed him into even heavier use of speed.

De Blanc became psychotic, claiming he was receiving messages from people on the moon. He put rifles in his car. Eventually he ended up in San Francisco General Hospital for twelve days.

Janis didn't end up in the hospital, but she wasn't far from it. She'd dwindled to just eighty-eight pounds. Chet Helms remembered that "she was emaciated . . . almost catatonic, just not responding. Things were happening and she could *not* respond. That's like terminal speed."[5]

> **"Janis returned home convinced that her past ways were wrong."**
> **—Laura Joplin**

But one day, while de Blanc was in the hospital, Janis told her friends, she woke up "and realized I was going to die."

She and Gottfried decided to quit speed. When Peter was released, they made plans. Gottfried would go to Hawaii to meet her boyfriend, Malcolm Wauldron. Janis would go to Port Arthur, away from the temptations of San Francisco . . . and prepare for her marriage to Peter de Blanc.

She arrived home in Port Arthur in May 1965.

A Strange Interlude

Janis's next few months in Port Arthur were, in a way, one of the most unusual interludes of her short life.

"Janis returned home convinced that her past ways were wrong. For the first time, she was asking for advice from our parents and listening to their replies. She was no longer passing through town, content with her way of life. She had come home to recoup and repair," wrote her sister, Laura.[6]

Janis returned to college, this time planning to study sociology instead of art. She enrolled in the second summer-school session at Lamar Tech, taking swimming, world history, and a survey of British Literature. She completely changed her way of dressing, wearing prim, practical dresses with long sleeves, despite the heat; Janis wanted to hide the needle tracks on her arms.

In August, Peter de Blanc came to visit. Janis knew from Linda Gottfried by then that de Blanc was already married and that his wife was pregnant, yet she still seemed convinced that somehow the two of them would be getting married. The family didn't know anything about his past, of course; in fact, he played the role of future son-in-law to the hilt, formally asking Seth Joplin for Janis's hand in marriage. Seth consented.

The family enjoyed de Blanc's company and was sorry when he said he had to return home to take care of family business. Suspiciously, in hindsight, he told the family he needed to get things "squared away," so he could announce the marriage properly. He asked

A photo of Janis taken in October, 1970.

that the Joplins not make any kind of formal announcement, either.

In reality, de Blanc had a new girlfriend, Debbie Boutellier, in New Orleans. De Blanc had met Boutellier on a trip to Mexico he had taken after Janis left San Francisco for Texas. De Blanc had told Boutellier he would break up with Janis while in Port Arthur.

But he didn't. Instead, he kept stringing her along with letters and phone calls.

When her father said he had given de Blanc consent to marry Janis, Laura wrote that Janis "jumped up and down, hugging Peter and clutching his steady arm as if it were a tether to reality."[7] After that, despite the misgivings she had about de Blanc, despite the pregnant wife she'd been told about, Janis began preparing for their life together.

She started a quilt for her trousseau. She went to Houston to visit Dave and Patti McQueen, and she and Patti bought china and linens and cutlery at Pier 1. In her calendar, she noted her parents' anniversary, other celebrations for other members of the family, and scrawled hearts and other symbols of love on the bottom of some of the pages, joining her name to Peter de Blanc's.

Janis Seeks Therapy

Janis also started therapy with Bernard Giarratano, a psychiatric social worker. "She said she wanted to be straight," Giarratano recalled. She wanted to meet her family's expectations for her. She idealized her

> **Not only had Janis been avoiding singing, she'd even been avoiding her old friends.**

father, whom she thought of as an intellectual— and, particularly, she wished she could be more like her younger sister, Laura.

Janis showed parts of her true self to Giarratano that she kept hidden from everyone else that summer. One day she even sang, something she'd been reluctant to do since she got back to Texas for fear it would lead her back into the jungle of drugs she was trying to escape.

Not only had Janis been avoiding singing, she'd even been avoiding her old friends, maybe afraid that their drinking would lead to her drinking too much again. When she did see them, she got after them for swearing and drinking so much.

But she didn't stay away from singing for long. She kept visiting local folk-music clubs, and over the Thanksgiving holiday in November 1965, she sang at the Half-Way House in Beaumont. By that time, Jim Langdon was writing a music column for the *Austin American-Statesman*. In his review of her performance, he called her the best blues singer in the country and expressed the hope that her status as relatively unknown would soon change.

Janis had originally expected Peter de Blanc to come down to Port Arthur for the holidays and bring her an engagement ring, but he called off the trip long before Christmas. He told a series of lies about all the problems he was having, when he was actually living in New York with Debbie Boutellier. He pretended to Janis when she would call him, and Debbie would pick up the phone, that Debbie was his cousin.

Some time in November or December, Janis seemed to have realized that the supposed wedding would never happen. She quit working on the quilt.

However, she continued living with the family, she even painted a Nativity mural for her mother that Christmas. In January 1966, she returned to school, studying math, industrial sociology, physical science, United States history, and the sociology of marriage.

She also resumed her active sex life, with both men and women. She made visits to Houston and Austin and continued to sing occasional gigs. Jim Langdon kept raving about her in his column, which helped her get additional singing jobs in Houston and Beaumont.

Burning for a Career

To her friends and family Janis did not show much ambition toward her career. But that wasn't what she told her counselor, Giarratano.

"She talked about it," he said. "She knew she wanted to do that. She did not know how it would fit in with the straight world, certainly not with her mother and dad." He said she was "burning" for a career, and he encouraged her to see if she could perform without falling into self-destructive behavior again.[8]

The possibility of self-destructive behavior was

A Janis Audition

Sometime in the first few months of 1966, Janis auditioned at a Houston place called Sand Mountain. Don Sanders, a well-known Texas folk musician, was there.

"Her face turned red and she kinda swung back and forth and whacked on her guitar and sang with all of her body," he said. "I was so shocked it didn't even make me critical. I had no reference point for it."

What shocked him the most, he said, was the way it "so powerfully crossed the gender line" as she sang a song with a male point of view, called "Winin' Boy," in a voice that sounded more like a male tenor's than a typical female folksinger's.[9]

precisely what concerned her mother. She was afraid music would lead Janis back into drugs.

Sometime during the year she spent in Port Arthur, Janis wrote "Turtle Blues," which talks about hiding. She seems to have been hiding in Port Arthur, but the call of music and her own talent eventually drew her out of her shell.

On March 5 and 6, 1966, Janis played a club in Austin called the Eleventh Door. James Langdon, one of the three boys she'd known back in high school had convinced her to sing a benefit concert. The crowd loved the white woman who sang with such a black-sounding voice and Joplin found her career as a singer back on track.[10]

A week later, Janis sang at a benefit concert for

Teodar Jackson, a blind fiddler who had become ill and had no money. Langdon emceed the event, and he wrote in his column that all of the performers were great, but Janis, the only female performer, "literally electrified the audience with her performance.

In May, she played a blues festival at the Texas Union Auditorium, sharing major billing with Robert Shaw. She had other gigs in Houston and Beaumont, and just like at the Eleventh Door, the crowd loved the white woman who sang with her black-sounding voice.

Janis Doesn't Come Home

When the summer break came around, Janis wrote to Jim Langdon, who got her another booking at the Eleventh Door. Janis headed to Austin, telling her parents she was just going up there for a week until summer school started.

But a week went by, and Janis didn't come home.

Her mother called Jim Langdon in Austin. Janis, he said, had gone back to California.

Dorothy Joplin was furious. "Without your influence, my daughter would still be at home!" she screamed at Langdon, ignoring his protestations that he had tried to talk Janis out of going.

Janis wrote her family on June 6, explaining what had happened. "When I got to Austin, I talked to Travis Rivers who gave me a spiel about my singing w/a band out here. Seems Chet Helms, old friend, now is Mr. Big in S.F. Owns 3 big working Rock & roll band with bizarre names like Captain Beefheart & his Magic Band,

Big Brother & the Holding Co. etc. Well, Big Brother et al. needs a vocalist. . . . "[10]

The family moved Janis's things into the den, hoping she'd be back in Port Arthur in the fall. But, of course, she wasn't.

"Janis had left us again," wrote her sister, Laura. "Away from the family and friends who knew and loved her, no one was there to call her hand when she went too far. Janis had come home and asked for help. She had been given all that any of us had to give. Still, her questions had gone unanswered."[11]

Chapter 5

Haight-Ashbury

San Francisco had changed a lot in the year Janis had been gone. The new center of artistic and other activity was no longer North Beach, but Haight-Ashbury, an area named after the two streets that intersected there. The days of everybody wearing black and the speed-soaked poetry readings of the beatniks had given way to everybody in tie-dyed shirts and the LSD-soaked ballroom dancing style of what the press would dub "hippies."

The new wave hit San Francisco on October 16, 1965, with a dance at the Longshoreman's Hall organized by the Family Dog production company. There was a light show. The Jefferson Airplane, the Great Society, and the Charlatans all played. Tickets were $2.50 for adults and $2 for students.

Hundreds of people showed up, some of whom had come to the Bay area for a big anti-Vietnam War demonstration in Oakland. Many of them were long-haired "freaks" (as they called themselves), and they were shocked to find so many other people like them.

Among those on hand: Chet Helms. Before long he would take over the promotion of the Family Dog dances himself.

Another promoter, Bill Graham, convinced by that dance and other similar events (some of which he staged) took out a four-year lease on the old Fillmore Auditorium. For a short time, he was partnered with Helms and John Carpenter, who managed the Great Society. Graham allowed Helms and Carpenter to use the venue every other weekend in exchange for telling him about the hot bands. But the partnership fell apart, and on April 22, 1966, Helms opened a rival to the Fillmore, the Avalon Ballroom, once part of a chain of ballrooms when swing music had been king. It even had a sprung wooden dance floor that would move in time to the dances.

Before he got into promoting dances, Helms had been promoting music, especially jam sessions in an old Victorian boardinghouse at 1090 Page Street that had its own basement ballroom with a separate street entrance. At one such jam session, a band began to form with Sam Andrew on guitar, Chuck Jones on drums, Peter Albin playing bass, and Paul Beck on vocals. Originally the group was called Blue Yard Hill.

Beck left the group before the end of 1965 and was replaced by a second guitarist, James Gurley. Helms managed the group, which began calling itself Big Brother and the Holding Company.

Big Brother played its first gig, which was almost entirely instrumental and improvised, in December 1965 at Berkeley's Open Theater. Not long after, it played at the Matrix, a club where a lot of bands got started. Local musicians who attended agreed that the biggest problems were Peter Albin's vocals and the fact the drummer couldn't keep time. Dave Getz soon replaced Chuck Jones on drums, forming the lineup that was in place when Janis arrived that spring.

Big Brother and the Holding Company became the "house band" at the Avalon Ballroom. They were one of a handful of early bands that formed the core of the new San Francisco music scene. The others were The Grateful Dead, Quicksilver Messenger Service, the Jefferson Airplane, and Country Joe and the Fish. Big Brother called what it played "freak rock." It was all about spontaneity; too much polish, too much professionalism, was frowned upon. "To the extent there was a 'San Francisco sound,' wrote biographer Alice Echols, "it consisted of extended jamming and soloing."

"We were just going for it," said Sam Andrew. "We had no musical knowledge. Actually, I was afraid to bring out what knowledge I had. It was very hard to show anyone anything then. Everyone wanted to arrive at whatever it was by experimentation."[1]

"The Perfect Person for Our Kind of Band"

With a drummer in place, the band members felt the remaining piece they needed to make Big Brother complete was a vocalist. Helms mentioned Janis. Peter Albin and James Gurley had known Janis in North Beach, and the others agreed she sounded perfect. Helms knew how to find her and how to lure her back to San Francisco.

She arrived there on June 4, and as soon as she met the band and practiced with them, they knew they'd made the right choice. "We knew we were gonna use her from the first time she opened her mouth and started singing," Peter Albin said. "We said, 'This is the perfect person for our kind of band.' "[2]

Just six days later, on June 10, she joined them onstage at the Avalon Ballroom.

Audience reaction was mixed. After all, Big Brother had its own cult following, and its fans didn't want the band changing to accommodate some strange Texan blues singer. But the band had no doubts.

Janis herself was pleased with her debut with Big Brother and the Holding Company. "I just exploded," she said. "I'd never sung like that before. I'd been into a Bessie Smith type thing. I stood still and I sang simple. But you can't sing like that in front of a rock band, all that rhythm and volume going. You have to sing loud and move wild with all that in back of you."[3]

Singing with Big Brother held its own special challenges beyond the fact it was a rock band. They were louder and faster than other bands. At first, Janis tried to keep up, but Sam Andrew thought that just made her sound like "a tape on fast forward."

In those early gigs, Janis only sang on about one third of the numbers. The rest of the time she'd stand in the back and play the tambourine. But when she sang, her sister, Laura, wrote: "Janis must have felt that the audience response was as much for her as for the music. This was the ultimate community she had sought to find or create since her break with convention at age fourteen. . . . They accepted her for her true self, her soul. They related to the real person that she was."[4]

Communal Living

In July, just a month after Janis arrived in San Francisco, she moved with the rest of the band to a large house in Lagunitas, where other rock bands had also moved. Away from the San Francisco nightlife, the band could focus on rehearsing and getting better.

It wasn't just the band living there: There were also the band members' wives and lovers, children, dogs, and cats.

James Gurley lived there with his wife, Nancy, and baby boy, Hongo, and Janis and Nancy became close, even though Janis and James Gurley had slept together and even lived together for a while.

Nancy was the "central figure in the Lagunitas house and the leader of its ceremonial rites," according to Myra Friedman. One of those rites was bead making, which Nancy taught all the other women to do. Unfortunately for Janis, Nancy also used speed.

"For a while, Janis held the line on drugs, with only occasional drinks of alcohol, but living in Lagunitas changed that," Laura Joplin wrote. "There were big parties, and lots of intoxicating and mind-expanding chemicals. So, she did some drugs. It wasn't the main focus of her life; she was just being part of the scene."[5]

But she didn't have any problem with the other major drug of the music scene in California at the time—alcohol. She later called Big Brother an "alcydelic" band, one fueled by both alcohol and LSD. According to James Gurley, everyone in the band needed a couple of shots of hard liquor before performing.

Despite the communal extended-family living arrangements, and despite painting the band's symbol (designed by a poster-artist called Mouse) on her car, Janis wasn't fully committed to Big Brother as far as her singing career went. The recording director of Elektra Records, Paul Rothchild, approached her about possibly joining a new blues roots band he was developing. She rehearsed with the band—made up of Taj Mahal, Stefan Grossman, and Al Wilson—without telling Big Brother.

When the other members of Big Brother found out, they accused her of betraying them. They argued that Big Brother was on the verge of making it. A small record company called ESP had already approached them about recording.

LSD

Dr. Albert Hoffman discovered lysergic acid diethyla-mide, aka LSD or acid, in 1938 while studying the ergot fungus, which grows on some grains and grasses and can be poisonous. When he accidentally dosed himself with it five years later, he discovered it gave him vivid hallucinations.

In the 1940s, Sandoz Pharmaceutical commercially marketed LSD. Canadian psychiatrists who tested it in the 1950s found that it could help cure alcoholism and might help treat schizophrenia. Dr. Humphrey Osmond, a British psychiatrist working at the mental hospital in Weyburn, Saskatchewan, coined the term *psychedelic* to describe the drug, which affected the mind rather than the body.

When recreational use of the drug became widespread, officials became alarmed, and the drug was outlawed in 1967. However, its use was so widespread in the counterculture of the 1960s that wild color schemes and strange, distorted images, reminiscent of LSD-fueled hallucinations, soon spread through mainstream culture, too, and were also dubbed "psychedelic." Today, the whole decade is sometimes known as the psychedelic sixties.

In the end, Janis agreed not to make a decision until after they went to Chicago. She wrote her family: "I'm just fraught w/indecision! And let's face it, I'm flattered. Rothchild said I was one of the 2 maybe 3 best female singers in the country & they want me. Well, what I'm hoping is the Chicago job will show me exactly how good Big Brother is . . . & then I can make up my mind."[6]

Big Brother in Chicago

The band arrived in Chicago without a manager. They'd let Chet Helms go because so much of his attention was devoted to the Avalon Ballroom instead of them. Chicago, they discovered, was not Haight-Ashbury. "People were eying us like they were going to beat us up," Dave Getz remembered. "White working-class people called us names on the streets. All the time, every day."[7]

They had a four-week engagement at a club called Mother Blues, which had switched to rock 'n' roll

Janis Joplin walks along Haight Street in 1967.

because there was too much competition from other blues clubs. Their music proved no more popular in Chicago than their far-out California clothes.

Nick Gravenites brought a record-producer friend of his, George McGowsky, to hear Big Brother. "Too bad she won't ever make it," McGowsky told Gravenites. "They're just too far out for the business."

The first two weeks of the four-week gig, the band still got paid: $1,000 a week. The third week, because Big Brother wasn't drawing enough customers, the club owner ran out of money. Peter Albin went to the Musician's Union, but the club owner simply didn't have any money to pay them . . . which left them stuck in Chicago with no way to go home.

That meant they were playing for gate receipts— whatever money was paid by audiences to see their show. Peter Albin said, "We had to start developing a stage show, with me doing a lot of witty remarks. But it still didn't come off. And finally, the last week, we . . . got a go-go girl. We named her Miss Proton, the Psyche-delic Girl." Miss Proton wore leotards covered with spray paint and glitter, and a hat made out of Saran Wrap.

In desperate straits, Big Brother was approached by a record producer named Bob Shad from Mainstream Records, for whom they had auditioned back in San Francisco. Chet Helms had rejected any offers Shad might have made then. But now, in Chicago, without Helms, they agreed to what was then a fairly standard contract giving them 5 percent of royalties—and the record company ownership of any songs they wrote.

That deal would come back to haunt them, but in the meantime the record offer convinced Janis to stick with Big Brother instead of joining Paul Rothchild's new blues band. She told Rothchild, however, that she'd decided to stay with Big Brother because she'd fallen in love with one of the guys in the band.

The First Record

Big Brother went into the studio and recorded four songs in one nine-hour session. Shad wanted songs that were radio-friendly, so his engineers refused to allow any of the recording meters to peak in the red zone during the recording. Band members worried that the cautious approach would fail to capture their shrieking guitar sound. But everyone was pleased with Janis's vocals, although in Chicago she mostly sang backup.

Big Brother—and especially Janis—continued to draw rave reviews locally.

Everyone except Peter Albin returned to San Francisco crammed with all their equipment into a borrowed car. (Albin's relatives bought him an airplane ticket.) They completed recording the album in Los Angeles a month later, and Janis was featured on all six remaining cuts.

Shad promised to release the first single in a month or two. But when it came out, "Blindman" was ignored. The B-side, "All Is Loneliness," didn't do any better.

The full album wasn't released until Janis became nationally famous. The band didn't make a penny from it.

Their record may not have taken off, but Big Brother—and especially Janis—continued to draw rave reviews locally and, as examples of the San Francisco hippie scene, even some national media attention. *Time* magazine, "the source that our family trusted weekly," as Laura Joplin called it, declared "The Younger Generation" its "Man of the Year" in 1966, and on December 16, 1966, mentioned Big Brother and the Holding Company as one of the numerous new rock groups that could be distinguished only by their "oddball names."

The chaos and conflict caused by everyone living together drove the band back into the Haight-Ashbury district in January 1967, when the lease on the Lagunitas house ran out.

"Something's Gonna Happen"

The district had changed. People from all over North America were heading to the coast, where, as Laura Joplin put it, "Hard-core hippies were beginning to make money being hippies! . . . They opened head shops (shops that sell drug-related paraphernalia) and clothing stores, and the profits gave the owners a living and the $2.50 cover charge at the Avalon Ballroom."

At the center of it all was the music. A county newspaper reported that Big Brother hoped "that the San Francisco sound makes the national scene, and

Folk singer Joan Baez sits at the corner of Haight and Ashbury giving a spontaneous concert in San Francisco in 1967.

that San Francisco becomes the Liverpool (birthplace of the Beatles) of the United States."

Janis said, "Something's gonna happen. It isn't just gonna go on. Either we're all gonna go broke and split up, or get rich and famous."

On January 4, 1967, twenty thousand people showed up for the "Human Be-In, a gathering of the tribes," held in Golden Gate Park on the polo field. Big Brother didn't play, but the Grateful Dead, Jefferson Airplane, and jazz trumpeter Dizzy Gillespie did. Timothy Leary was there, with his slogan: Turn on, tune in, drop out. He said he was trying to form a religion based on the psychedelic experience of LSD. Allen Ginsberg chanted poems. And just about everyone took acid.

Linda Gravenites, ex-wife of Nick Gravenites, thought the Be-In marked the moment when Haight-Ashbury went from something spontaneous and real to "a hyped-up caricature," thanks to the press coverage, which focused on sex, drugs, and rock 'n' roll.

The counterculture took on a darker edge, said Gravenites. "Up until then, people came because they were full to overflowing and were sharing their fullness. After that, it was the empties who came, wanting to be filled."[8]

In March of 1967, Linda Gravenites moved in with Janis Joplin, and they became good friends. Linda designed clothes for boutiques and costumes for the theater, and she began designing clothes for Janis: shiny pants, low-cut blouses, flowers in her hair. Big Brother had a job on the movie *Petulia* that month, and Janis sought out photographer Stanley Ciccone, begging him to tell her how to use makeup artistically.

Romantically around that time Janis hooked up with Country Joe McDonald, leader of the band Country Joe and the Fish. The romance ended a short while later because the two were more interested in pursuing their personal goals than having a relationship.

Clashes Within the Band

Janis's ambition had grown, and she clashed with Peter Albin over both their respective roles within Big Brother and the style of stage shows they were performing. Before Janis arrived, James Gurley and his unique, lightning-fast guitar playing had been the star, but now Janis was beginning to draw more attention. In fact, people were telling her she was better than the rest of the band.

People were telling her she was better than the rest of the band.

Albin, meanwhile, had been the one who talked to the audience between songs and conducted the day-to-day business. Under Musician's Union rules, he was also entitled to an extra 20 percent of the group's earnings because he signed their union contracts.

At a group meeting, Janis complained about that, claiming that since she was doing more for the band than anyone else, she should be the one signing the contracts. An angry Albin told her he'd never taken an extra dime, because in Big Brother everything was shared.

Janis also preferred a more traditional kind of talking to the audience, where the focus was on the next song, whereas Albin acted more like a stand-up comic, and sometimes even did things like guiding the audience in breathing exercises.

After Chet Helms, Big Brother was without a manager for a while. Jim Kalarney took over that role for a short period, and then in January 1967, Julius Karpen became manager. He held a high opinion of Big Brother.

The band continued working hard on their music, rehearsing daily in a warehouse on Van Ness Street. "There was a lot of input from everyone about the music," according to Bob Gordon, the band's attorney. "There was real good genuine cooperation. . . ."[9]

Karpen even sent Janis for formal voice lessons, although he had to coax her to go and call her to be sure she went.

All the work paid off where it counted: on stage. In the *San Francisco Examiner* on March 22, Philip Elwood wrote: "Most dynamic of the musical performers is granny-gowned Janice [sic] Joplin with Big Brother. . . ."[10]

The band was tight, Janis was hot, everything was in place for a big breakout . . . and right on cue, here came the Monterey Pop Festival.

Chapter 6

To Monterey and Beyond!

The Human Be-In in January inspired a lot of wannabe hippies from across the country to come to San Francisco. It also inspired a booking agent named Ben Shapiro and his partner, Alan Pariser. They decided to organize a festival that would showcase the new style of rock 'n' roll music. For a venue, they chose the Monterey County Fairgrounds, located eighty miles south of San Francisco.

Shapiro and Pariser joined forces with John Phillips of the Mamas and the Papas and that group's producer, Lou Adler. Phillips, who had started in folk music, convinced Shapiro to make the new festival artist-run and nonprofit like the famous Newport Folk Festival. Shortly after that, Adler and Phillips bought out Shapiro.

Adler convinced ABC-TV to film the event (and pay $400,000 for the privilege) and signed up a number of Los Angeles groups, including the Beach Boys, the Byrds, the Buffalo Springfield, and, of course, the Mamas and the Papas, even though, because it was a nonprofit festival, musicians were only to be paid their expenses.

Adler and Phillips had more trouble signing up the bands in San Francisco, who generally had no use for the L.A. brand of music or the L.A. way of doing business. In the end, though, with the help of a board composed of musicians that included Paul McCartney, Paul Simon, and Smokey Robinson, the San Francisco bands joined on.

The Monterey Pop Festival ran for two and a half days, featured twenty-five hours of music, had forty thousand people in attendance, and was almost problem

Fans at a concert in Livermore, California, on December 8, 1969.

free. Twelve hundred journalists attended the festival. That and the ABC-TV filming of the event ensured that an outstanding performance there would make waves across the country.

Which is just what happened. When all the dust (and marijuana smoke) had cleared, one band and three individuals were considered the undisputed stars of the festival: Jimi Hendrix, demonstrating his showmanship and astonishing guitar playing to a large U.S. audience for the first time; The Who (Pete Townshend of The Who smashed his guitar, Jimi Hendrix smashed and burned his); Otis Redding, who had a tight, polished act completely different from what the laid-back hippie bands offered, but whose singing was so powerful nobody cared; and Janis Joplin.

Getting National Attention

Big Brother had been scheduled for Saturday afternoon—hardly prime time—because they weren't considered a big draw. But they understood the importance of their appearance to the audience. Janis called her friend (and, later, lover) Peggy Caserta, who owned a clothing boutique in San Francisco. Caserta suggested she wear her peace dress, which was a plain shift covered with peace symbols, but in the end, Janis wore a pair of denim jeans and a simple top. Caserta also told Janis to sing as if it were her only chance.

Janis did.

The band played "Down on Me," "Road Block," and "Ball and Chain."

Rock critic Michael Lydon wrote: "In great shouts that send her strings of beads flying and knot her face into grimaces, the energy explodes and explodes again, sending out waves of electrical excitement."[1]

Just like that, Big Brother—or more specifically, Janis—had national attention.

Lou Adler was stunned when he and the other promoters discovered none of Janis's amazing performance had been filmed. Because nothing had been offered to the band for film rights, Karpen had ensured that the ABC-TV cameras were all pointed to the ground during Big Brother's set.

The band was furious. So were the promoters. Janis went to Albert Grossman, the "hippest, shrewdest manager of all," manager of, among others, Bob Dylan, and with his help the band convinced Karpen to let them perform a second set on Sunday night, which would be filmed. Because of that incident, Julius Karper didn't work with Big Brother and the Holding Company again.

Just like that, Big Brother—or more specifically, Janis—had national attention. The major newsmagazines, *Time* and *Newsweek*, and newspapers from the *Los Angeles Times* to the *Houston Post* wrote about Janis as the star of the Monterey Pop Festival.

It cemented the shift that had begun that placed Janis at the center of the band instead of James Gurley, Peter Albin, or any of the others. From that point on, all

A Visit From the Family

Janis's family—Dorothy, Seth, Michael, and Laura—visited her in Haight-Ashbury in August 1967. Janis "was giddy with excitement," Laura wrote, showing off her favorite shops and ballrooms, the colorful clothing, her apartment—and that night at the Avalon Ballroom, her music.

Laura remembered that "the room was dark, but the lack of regular light was overpowered by the light show of moving colors and images on the wall. People sat immobile and stared, not necessarily at anything, just ahead. Their heads moved slowly. . . . Big Brother performed a few tunes, working in synchronized fashion with the swirling lights to force the viewer's attention into the present."

She added, "We didn't stay long after Janis performed, not finding a way to relate to the scene. . . . I am sure that after that experience, our parents ceased believing that they could influence her or that she would return to Texas and college. . . . .

"She asked, 'Oh, can't you see?' She stood, staring at us walking down the street, with the roar of the rock music pouring forth from . . . the ballroom. Caught between two worlds, she stood, perplexed, believing that we should like it. I think Janis realized then that we didn't, and couldn't, and probably weren't going to see."[2]

anyone wanted to talk about with regard to Big Brother was Janis and the way she could sing.

Albert Grossman Takes Over

When Karpen began managing the band in January of 1967, they earned $400 for a two-night weekend. By the end of 1967, they earned $2,500 a night—and they still hadn't released a major album. However, the material they'd recorded in Chicago and Los Angeles for Mainstream Records suddenly started coming out as singles after Janis's amazing Monterey performance. It appeared in a record album titled *Big Brother and the Holding Company* in August, as Mainstream tried to capitalize on all the Monterey buzz.

Big Brother's contract with Mainstream was a problem. Clive Davis, the new president of Columbia Records, wanted the band, but first that five-year exclusive contract had to be dealt with.

It didn't happen until the band changed managers. Problems with Julius Karpen came to a head after Karpen refused to let Big Brother open for the Jefferson Airplane and the Grateful Dead at the Hollywood Bowl late in the year, because he felt Big Brother should be the headline act. Bill Graham, the promoter of the concert, phoned each band member individually and told them that Karpen was hurting their careers. Karpen refused to let them inspect the accounting books. In the end, he left. But it soon became clear that there weren't any books, just piles of unorganized receipts. Not only that, Dave Getz said that Karpen lost the band's earnings in a bad investment.

The band needed a *good* manager. Several people suggested Albert Grossman, who had helped them get the encore performance at Monterey. Although based in New York, Grossman came out to San Francisco to discuss the possibility with them, and he agreed to take them on.

Grossman had managed a number of blues artists and both created and managed the group Peter, Paul, and Mary. But his greatest claim to fame was as the manager of superstar Bob Dylan.

Grossman was known as a shrewd businessman and someone with an eye and ear for talent. When he came to talk to Big Brother, the band members asked him if he would guarantee a yearly income.

"Name a figure," he said, and someone suggested seventy-five thousand dollars. "Make it a hundred thousand and I'll put it in writing," Grossman replied. "If I can't make you that, I'm in the wrong business." Among his conditions was that none of the band members could be heroin users.[3]

Big Brother and the Holding Company signed with Albert Grossman on November 11, 1967. Now, at last, they had someone who could get them out of the contract with Mainstream records. Grossman eventually convinced CBS Records to buy out the Mainstream contract for $250,000, with only half of that amount to be recovered from Big Brother's future royalties on record sales.

In the meantime, Grossman put everything about the band on a more professional level. On December 1, John Cooke, a former Harvard student and Boston folk musician, was hired as the band's road manager. (Cooke had his choice of acts, and chose Big Brother.)

The band didn't take to him at once, but within a few months, they found him indispensable. He looked after travel arrangements, pushed people to be on time, organized the equipment, and kept tabs on the gate receipts.

Outshining the Band

Janis's star continued to rise and outshine that of the band as a whole. The *San Francisco Examiner* included her in a fashion spread in October. She received fan letters from men claiming they had hunted for a woman like Janis forever.

She had no shortage of lovers, thanks to her new-found fame. "Before she was famous, people

> **Janis's star continued to rise and outshine that of the band as a whole.**

didn't think Janis was attractive . . . and now she had all these admirers," said Peggy Caserta.[4]

One story has it that Jimi Hendrix had sex with Janis Joplin backstage in a dressing room, but Linda Gravenites says it was actually she with Jimi that night. Janis definitely spent a night with Jim Morrison of The Doors. They didn't get along after that, though. Months later, Janis hit Morrison over the head with a whiskey bottle after he grabbed her hair during an argument.

Another boyfriend was a Hell's Angel nicknamed Freewheelin' Frank. There were many others.

For Christmas of 1967, Janis went home to Port Arthur, bearing presents, especially lots of copies of Big Brother's single "Down on Me." A reporter-photographer from the *Port Arthur News* came by to interview her.

When she returned to San Francisco, Janis discovered she was pregnant. She flirted with the idea of keeping the baby, but in the end she decided that was impossible and went to Mexico for an abortion.

The procedure wasn't done properly, and at a club in Los Angeles, Big Brother's booking agent, Todd Schiffman, found Janis doubled over in agonizing pain in the dressing room. She told him she'd had an abortion two days earlier and asked him to help her to a phone so she could call the hospital.

The club had been taken over by organized crime, and the owners had sabotaged the public-address system in retaliation. Schiffman suggested she use that as an excuse for not going on and she agreed. But once she was on stage, she found thousands of people waiting and the public-address system working again.

Even though Schiffman said he literally "picked her up off the floor and almost carried her down the hall," instead of begging off, she said, "There's a lot . . . going down here tonight. There are guys backstage walking around with guns and all. But, you know, you're here and I'm here and we're going to do it."

Schiffman remembered, "I couldn't believe it. She put on an hour show and you wouldn't have known she was sick. I couldn't believe my eyes. That tells us what kind of dedication and craziness she had."[5]

"She Tore the Place Apart"

The next month, on February 17, 1968, Big Brother hit the East Coast for the first time, playing the Anderson Theater in New York City, the headline act on a bill that included blues guitarist B. B. King.

B. B. King had never before played to a downtown white audience. They loved him, demanding seven or eight encores. "Janis was terrified to follow him," remembered musician John Morris, who had spent most of the afternoon with Janis and was backstage before the show. "She didn't want to go on . . . "

But she did go on. "She tore the place apart," said Morris. "She had 'em. I'd never seen a performance like that in my life. Before that curtain went up she was a scared little girl, she wasn't 'Janis Joplin' . . . I think I've done about four hundred concerts in my life, and probably seen eight hundred, and that would have to rank with the top two or three of all of them."[6]

During their eight weeks in New York on that first East Coast trip, the band also signed their new contract with CBS's Columbia Records label. Press coverage of the trip was favorable . . . and focused almost exclusively on Janis. In a letter home on April 4, 1968, Janis listed some of the magazines and newspapers that were doing stories: *Vogue, Glamour, The New York*

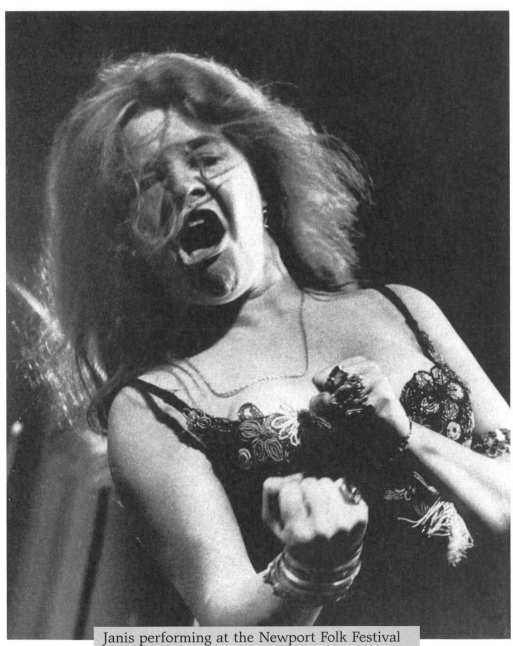

Janis performing at the Newport Folk Festival with Big Brother and the Holding Company on July 29, 1968.

Times, Jazz & Pop, Eye, Life, New York Magazine, Cashbox, Billboard, Record World, Variety, Village Voice, and several underground papers. "They wrote as though Janis were a singer with a band backing her and not the family-unit San Francisco band," Laura Joplin wrote.

And Grossman's office changed the billing from "Big Brother and the Holding Company" to "Big Brother and the Holding Company, featuring Janis Joplin."

Album Angst

Big Brother needed to record an album. On March 1 and 2 they played the Grande Ballroom in Detroit, intending to make a live recording, but they got nothing they considered useable.

They returned to New York to try recording in the studio but continued to struggle. The incredible press and public attention that had erupted after their New York debut continued. "The press had gone absolutely amok, seized by a delirium of enthusiasm and palpitating with an extravagance of language as reckless and abandoned as Janis's own performances and her outrageous façade," wrote Myra Friedman, who was right in the middle of the media whirlwind, managing interview requests as the band's press agent.[7]

She made it clear that it all happened with a minimum of effort from Grossman's office: no flood of press releases, no phone calls to the press, no staged events. "Janis Joplin was the only pop singer in history to become a superstar without even having what could be called a record!" Friedman wrote. "Preceded by such heated expectations, the quality of that recording would be more crucial than would ordinarily be the case."

Filmmaker D. A. Pennebaker, who had filmed the Monterey Pop Festival and done a film on Bob Dylan called *Don't Look Back,* had agreed to do a film on Janis similar to the one he'd done on Dylan. He captured some of the studio work. At one point, Janis defied producer John Simon, a former jazz musician with perfect pitch. He wanted the band to do take after take in an effort to get it perfect, but Janis said, "What you hear is what's up front and that's the vocal. Unless the instrumental really makes a mistake you aren't gonna hear it." Of course, by saying that, she also insulted the band members.[8]

But, in fact, she was right. Fred Catero, the engineer, said the vocals worked fine, but the instrumental parts always had mistakes, to the point that Janis once stormed out of the studio after four tries to record a particular song.

The band, wrote Alice Echols, was "trying to record music of the moment for a producer who believed records should be forever." As a result, two weeks of recording in New York netted only three songs, and it eventually took another month in a Los Angeles studio to finish the LP.

The band didn't think Simon understood their music. Simon, for his part, was frustrated with the band's lack of professionalism in the studio. "I always thought they were a great *performance* band, but I *didn't* think they made it as a recording band," he said. "The drugs! That's how Janis Joplin could happen in the first place. Everyone's mind was fried! . . . You know, there's studied music and there's tribal music and their stuff leaned more toward tribal music."[9]

The struggles in the studio created strife between Janis and Big Brother.

After a thirty-six-hour marathon mixing session involving the whole band, Big Brother's first album, called *Cheap Thrills*, was finished. They had originally wanted to call it *Sex, Dope and Cheap Thrills*, but Columbia had refused to let them use the first two words. It featured caricatures of the band by under-ground comic artist R. Crumb on the cover. John Simon was not involved as his original mix had been rejected by Columbia, and he had already committed to move on to another project.

> **The struggles in the studio created strife between Janis and Big Brother.**

Cheap Thrills came out in August 1968. Reviews were mixed, but the album sold a million copies in its first month.

Despite its success, though, Janis's days with Big Brother and the Holding Company were numbered.

The Divide Deepens

Throughout 1968, the press continued to focus on Janis Joplin while more or less ignoring the band. There were a few really negative reviews of the band and Janis both, but not very many. The attention made Janis fabulously successful—but separated her more and more from her bandmates and maybe even from reality. Her sister wrote that it separated her from the person she had once been.

"Her popular acceptance wouldn't have been possible had her public persona not been based on some true aspect of her personality," wrote Laura. "It was part of her, but she seemed to begin to believe it was all of her."[10]

> "If you're onstage and it's really working and you've got the audience with you, it's a oneness you feel."
> —Janis Joplin

The only time she was really herself, Laura (and others) thought, was when she was onstage. Onstage, she said, "I'm full of emotion and want a release. And if you're onstage and it's really working and you've got the audience with you, it's a oneness you feel."[11]

It was hard for Janis and the members of Big Brother to descend to reality after performing before audiences so wild about Janis that they would rush the stage. Their solution to the problem was drugs.

Janis's "drug of choice" was always alcohol. Her drink of choice, by 1968, was Southern Comfort, a sweet mixture of peach, orange, vanilla, cinnamon, sugar—and whisky. She usually had a bottle of it onstage as she performed.

But she wasn't averse to other drugs. The band would occasionally shoot up heroin. "Every couple of months we might come across some heroin," Sam Andrew remembered. "It was always after the show. It was a spirit of adventure and Janis got into doing things other people weren't."[12]

Sam Andrew was the one Janis first confided to, in June 1968, that she was thinking of leaving Big Brother. He didn't say anything to anyone. In September, she talked to him again about having a different kind of band, one with a horn section. She wanted him to be part of the new band. She also talked to Dave Getz at one point about continuing with her in a new band, and Nick Gravenites recalled Janis begging him to ask Albert Grossman if he would manage her separately.

Good-bye to Big Brother

Whatever the reason, Janis finally decided to leave Big Brother and the Holding Company. The official press release went out in mid-September, less than a month after *Cheap Thrills* was released. The press release said the band was unable to generate any new material, and Janis had been "pretending" onstage.

The band had heard well before that. They'd expected it, but Peter Albin still accused her of being a backstabber. The remaining band members met to plan out a new future for the group, but suffered another blow when Sam Andrew announced he was going with Janis to form a new band.

Despite the announcement, and resulting tension before, after, and even during concerts, the band performed constantly in the fall of 1968. At the Newport Folk Festival, Janis was excited to be on the same bill as Kenneth Threadgill, her old friend who owned the bar she had sung in, in Austin. She also met Kris Kristofferson there.

Big Brother's final concert with Janis was on December 1, 1968. Appropriately, it was a benefit for the

Big Brother and the Holding Company, featuring Janis Joplin performing on the set of *Petulia* in 1968.

Family Dog company. Chet Helms and his partners had been forced out of the Avalon Ballroom because of a noise complaint. The benefit helped Family Dog try again in a new location, but it soon failed.

Many San Francisco fans felt like an era was ending, and they saw Janis's split with Big Brother as another sign.

The San Francisco psychedelic ballroom scene, it seemed, was over. Many San Francisco fans felt like an era was ending, and they saw Janis's split with Big Brother as another sign. There was even graffiti in the Haight-Ashbury district reading: "Janis, please don't leave Big Brother."

Just three weeks after Big Brother's final concert, on December 21, 1968, Janis Joplin performed in public for the first time with her new group.

Chapter 7

Kozmic Blues

Janis wanted to move her career in a new direction.
She formed a corporation called Fantality (a combination
of fantasy and reality, much like her own life), and a
publishing company called Strong Arm Music. She had
a new, much more expensive wardrobe. And she had a
new band, put together with the help of Michael
Bloomfield and Nick Gravenites, featuring a rhythm-
and-blues sound, complete with horns. According to
Laura Joplin, Janis wanted to be like the great black soul
singer Aretha Franklin.

The new band played for fifteen minutes in Memphis
as the next-to-last act at the second annual Stax-Volt
Yuletide Thing, a Christmas party put on by Stax Records.
The record company's nickname was "Soulsville, USA."
Stax was most famous as the label of Otis Redding, who
had been killed in an airplane crash the year before.

Janis and the new, unnamed band were the second-
to-last act on a bill that otherwise featured only black

musicians. "The black half of the audience had little idea of who she was," Laura wrote. "They weren't familiar with her or most of her material. . . . There was little applause and no encore."[1]

Record producer Elliot Mazer said what he remembered most about the rehearsals with the band in New York was Janis's acute feelings of inferiority. "She'd *always* say, 'Did I do it well? Do you love me?' And when one's thinking about someone like Janis Joplin, you don't expect them to be *that* concerned. It was her constant fear that she'd look bad behind a bunch of good musicians."[2]

But the real test would come on February 11 at the Fillmore East in New York, the city she had taken by storm the first time she performed there with Big Brother.

Janis went home to Port Arthur for Christmas, then plunged back into rehearsals.

The New Band Kicks Off Its Tour

On February 11, 1969, the national press came out in force for the kickoff of the new band's tour. The Fillmore East sold out four performances. *Time, Life, Look,* and *Newsweek* reporters were there. So were Mike Wallace and a crew from *60 Minutes*, filming a segment called "Carnegie Hall for Kids."

That night, the new band consisted of Sam Andrew on lead guitar, Terry Clements on tenor sax, Richard Kermode on organ, Roy Markowitz on drums, Terry Hensley on trumpet, and "Keith Cherry" on bass. They played a few old songs of Big Brother's ("Piece of My Heart," "Ball and Chain," and "Summertime") but also two new songs and some covers of other artists' songs, including the Bee Gees' "To Love Somebody."

Audiences liked the performances, and the press response wasn't horribly negative. Generally, critics liked Janis (as usual) but felt the new band hadn't quite gelled.

Janis put her insecurities on display in a postshow interview with Paul Nelson of *Rolling Stone*. Nelson found it disconcerting to be talking to a star of Janis's caliber and be constantly asked for reassurance that she actually was good. "One gets the alarming feeling that Joplin's whole world is precariously balanced on what happens to her musically, that the necessary degree of honest cynicism needed to survive an all-media assault may be buried too far under an immensely likeable but tremendously under confident naiveté," he wrote. His article was headlined: *"Janis: The Judy Garland of Rock?"*[3]

Two weeks later in San Francisco, both audience and press reaction was much worse. Critic Ralph Gleason even suggested Janis should scrap her new band and go back to Big Brother.

In part, the reaction in San Francisco was due to the ongoing fallout from her decision to leave Big Brother, which the San Francisco press treated as a sellout. As far as they were concerned Janis had rejected the scene that had made her famous.

Myra Friedman wrote that, with the formation of the new band made up of professional musicians instead of a group of friends who had come together organically, "everything around Janis took a jarring shift into super show business gear."[4] In the press, Janis didn't talk about San Francisco and the movement any longer, but only about herself.

Janis often talked about living for the moment and not caring about the future, but, wrote Friedman, she was incredibly frugal with her finances, and she kept a scrupulous accounting of the money she spent and where it went.

A Near-Lethal Combination

But if she took good care of her financial future, she risked her own future all the time. Her use of heroin increased when the band went out to the West Coast to face a more hostile press and public, and she drank constantly. Combining heroin and alcohol can be lethal, causing the lung tissues to swell with water and breathing to stop. One day in March 1969, Linda Gravenites found Janis lying on the floor, turning purple. Linda forced her to her feet, and kept her walking until 3:00 A.M.

That same month, Janis performed on the *Ed Sullivan Show* to wild applause.

The band got a boost when it toured Europe in April 1969. Musically it was more together, and the European audiences didn't care about Janis's breakup with Big Brother.

A concert in Frankfurt for U.S. GIs drew two thousand people. A former soldier remembered that the audience "screamed, they loved her," and Janis called people up on stage "to feel and touch and love her. They filled the stage, leaving only a horse-shoe area for her to perform in."[5]

The audience in Albert Hall, London, got up and danced, even though Janis and the band had been warned that British audiences were far too reserved for that sort of thing. But Janis managed to break through the British reserve. Audience members really responded to Janis.

That same night, in a mirror image of the incident in San Francisco the month before, Linda Gravenites and Janis had to keep Sam Andrew alive after he overdosed on heroin at the postshow party. They put him in the bathtub, in ice-cold water, and kept jostling him to keep him awake.

Nor did Janis learn anything from the death of James Gurley's wife, Nancy, of an overdose of heroin, which Janis heard about when she returned to New York. Because James had injected Nancy, he was charged with murder. The reaction of Janis and Sam Andrew to the news reveals a lot about the way heroin dulls feeling: They went out and got some heroin of their own and shot it up.

Not long after that, Janis fired Sam Andrew from her band. She did it while they were both stoned on heroin.

"A Mess, a Total Mess"

Back in the United States, Janis and the band, plagued with constantly shifting personnel and still nameless, faced audiences far less enthused than the Europeans. "Performing, one of Janis's many drugs, was failing her," noted Alice Echols, who quotes Janis as saying, "You know, I have to have the *umph*. I've got to *feel* it, because if it's not getting through to me, the audience sure . . . aren't going to feel it either."[6]

According to Myra Friedman, by the time the band went into Columbia's studios in Hollywood in June to record a new Janis Joplin album, "it was just about ready for embalmment."

Bassist Brad Campbell said the sessions "were chaos. Everybody was putting down everybody else. It was a mess, a total mess."[7]

The producer of the new album, Gabriel Mekler, tended to ignore the suggestions of the band's experienced musicians. The engineer, Sye Mitchell, came on board after Janis verbally abused the original engineer, Jerry Hochman, so much that he quit.

> **"You know, I have to have the *umph*. I've got to *feel* it."**
> **— Janis Joplin**

The band spent ten days making the recording, and then went on the road. The band was supposed to come back and finish recording, but it never did.

The resulting album was titled *I Got Dem Ol' Kozmic Blues Again, Mama* (*Kozmic Blues*, for short). Critical response was, once again, mixed. *Kozmic Blues* went gold, but it had no Top 10 singles.

Then, in August 1969, Janis Joplin and her band

(which she called the Band from Beyond while touring in the East in July but later named the Kozmic Blues Band) played Woodstock, the giant music festival that became the symbol of the 1960s.

Woodstock

Half a million people turned out in a muddy farmer's field in rural New York. People were wet and miserable, the performances were disorganized and late, the sound system was inadequate, and some musicians received only half as much money they'd been promised. Woodstock may have earned its reputation as a great outpouring of love and good vibrations mainly because, despite the hardships, no one rioted.

For some musicians, Woodstock was a triumph. Jimi Hendrix's performance of "The Star-Spangled Banner" as the sun rose, captured on film, became a defining moment of the 1960s. But it wouldn't be a triumph for Janis.

She went on between the Grateful Dead and Sly and the Family Stone. She turned in a couple of good songs, but at one point her voice broke.

"Everything upset Janis that weekend—her band, her singing, the vastness of the event, and the fact that neither the audiences nor her fame were working for her anymore," wrote Alice Echols.[8]

Things went a little better on the weekend of August 30, 31, and September 1, when Janis played the Texas International Pop Festival at the Dallas International Motor Speedway in Lewisville, Texas. She received

Two concert-goers sit on the roof of
a Volkswagen bus at Woodstock.

several standing ovations. Shortly after that, she went home to Port Arthur for a brief visit, taking along her black saxophone player, Snooky Flowers. According to Laura Joplin, Flowers was the first black man entertained in the Joplin home, "a milestone of sorts, although it just felt like a friend coming over." Flowers took Janis down to Houston Avenue in Port Arthur to visit some of the local black clubs and meet the local black population, "which had been denied to her as a young girl."

Laura continued, "She elatedly confided to me, 'We talked to this really together old black lady who's seen it all, and she said I'm "really down," man, "down"! I can't believe it!' Janis needed acceptance from black society, from those whom her high-school friends had defined as the heroes of the underbelly of America, the guideposts of her life."[9]

Arrested in Florida

But things weren't going well. Janis's star continued to soar, with appearances on national television programs like *The Dick Cavett Show* and *This Is Tom Jones*, and constant attention from major media outlets.

And always, there was alcohol and heroin. In Houston, her old friend Philip Carter visited her backstage before a concert. He was astonished she could even perform, given how much alcohol she drank. After the concert, he saw her shoot up in her hotel room. He sent her a letter that read, "Janis, you're my friend and I wish you would stop hurting my friend."

But Janis seemed to think she was invincible. After an overdose killed an actor she knew, she told Linda Gravenites, "Well, some people die and some people are survivors. I'm a survivor."

But, wrote Myra Friedman, when Janis came back to New York, where she was based from October to December, "So far as I was concerned, she might as well have been slumped, nodding out in a public doorway, for all the resemblance to her former self that remained as the days went by."[10]

It seemed her concerts were no longer about music. The point was to get attention, to get the audience dancing, jumping, yelling, shrieking.

She encouraged crowds to get on their feet and dance. It got her in trouble on November 16, 1969, in Tampa, Florida. All over the country, police and fire-fighters were worried about the fire hazard and the possibility of people getting trampled as rock stars began playing city-owned arenas and auditoriums. That night in Tampa, nervous police started moving fans out of the aisles and away from the stage. When one of them came onto the stage with a bullhorn in the middle of a song to order people back to their seats, Janis swore at him over the microphone. She finished the song, but the hall managers cut the power and turned on the lights.

Janis swore at the cop with the bullhorn again as she left the stage, and she continued swearing at the police backstage, the incident ending with her being arrested and charged with two counts of vulgar and indecent language. Janis told reporters, "I say anything I want onstage. I don't mind getting arrested because I've turned on a lot of kids."[11]

Janis Sees a Doctor

Through the joint efforts of Albert Grossman, Linda Gravenites (back from London just the day before the incident in Tampa), and Myra Friedman, Janis was finally convinced to try to do something about her alcohol and heroin use. She went to see Dr. Edmund Rothschild, a doctor Albert Grossman had sent clients to before.

Janis told Dr. Rothschild that she used heroin after a concert. (That struck him as unusual. Most heroin users use the narcotic to escape psychological pain, but Janis used it when she was already "high" from the adulation she received in concert.) She considered her more serious problem to be her alcohol use, and the doctor agreed. He also found that she had a terrible diet, full of junk food and sweets.

Her lab tests showed that her liver function was normal. "Well, that just shows I'm really a strong, healthy person, because the way I've been drinking you'd think my liver would be shot!" she said.

Dr. Rothschild apparently found her very difficult to deal with. "One of her problems was that intellectually she was so advanced and her emotions were childlike and uncontrollable. . . . She couldn't be quiet. She was unbelievably 'on' most of the time," he said.[12]

She did try to cooperate a little bit, though. She went

Janis Joplin gives a victory sign as she leaves police headquarters with her attorney, Herbert Goldburg, in Tampa, Fl. She had been charged with two counts of vulgar and indecent language after police stopped her concert.

Janis Joplin performing with her band in December, 1969.

on methadone for a few days. Methadone stops the craving addicts feel and prevents them from feeling pleasure from heroin. But to really get off of heroin, addicts also need a new social group, one that encourages staying off of the drug rather than one that encourages its use.

Janis and her heroin-addicted friend Pat "Sunshine" Nichols agreed to both quit using heroin, and to not see each other until both of them were clean.

On December 19, 1969, the day after her methadone prescription ran out, Janis performed in Madison Square Garden. At the lavish party after the concert put on by Clive Davis, Friedman wrote: "Janis's face had a green-white glow, translucent or waxen or something like that, similar to the skin of a corpse," suggesting that just one day after the methadone ran out, Janis had returned to heroin.

"She seemed in bad shape," John Cooke recalled, and thought, "Gee, am I glad I left the tour when I did. I didn't want to watch this happen to her."[13]

Good-bye Kozmic Blues, Hello Brazil

The Madison Square Garden concert was the last concert played by the Kozmic Blues Band and Janis's last concert of 1969.

The next day she returned to California and settled into a new house in Larkspur. She threw a big housewarming party in the house, made cozy by a redwood interior, sliding glass doors, and surrounding pine woods. "Her house was nice, tasteful," is how Nick Gravenites described it, "not over- or underdone. . . . She loved her home and her dogs."

Still trying to kick heroin, Janis decided to go with Linda Gravenites to Brazil for Carnival, the plan being that they would have a good time without heroin, and when they came back, Janis would be clean.

The vacation, wrote Myra Friedman, was "spectacular." After a few days, Janis and Linda hooked up with American David Niehaus and his friend Ben Beall. Niehaus, originally from Cincinnati, had been in the Peace Corps in Turkey at one point and since then had traveled all over the world. He and Janis spent several weeks together, traveling down the coast to the city of Salvador. Janis liked the fact that Niehaus didn't even know who she was at first, and when he found out, it didn't matter.

Janis and Niehaus's involvement almost ended in disaster when they were in a motorcycle accident, but Janis only suffered a concussion.

Janis really did kick her heroin habit during her weeks in Brazil with Niehaus. They planned to go back to California together, but the passport check at the airport discovered Niehaus had overstayed his visa. Janis screamed obscenities at the

> **Janis liked the fact that Niehaus didn't even know who she was at first.**

officials, which didn't help. They sent her off on her flight, but kept Niehaus for two days.

Janis reacted by scoring some heroin in Los Angeles during a plane change. When she landed in San Francisco, she was already stoned.

Niehaus was shocked to find her back on heroin when he arrived. Her rock star lifestyle didn't suit him either. "Every time we went out of the house she had five hundred people screaming around her car," he said.[14]

They had some good times in California, but Niehaus hated the drugs (the alcohol he thought he could live with). Then, one day after returning to Larkspur from skiing, he discovered Janis in bed with her old friend and lover Peggy Caserta.

A photo of Janis taken in October of 1970.

David told Janis he couldn't stay. Janis suggested he become her road manager when she got her new band up and running and on tour. But what David really wanted was for her to come with him as he resumed his travels.

"David really loved her," according to Linda Gravenites. "Janis loved him too, but she was never satisfied. Even that, somebody loving her with all their heart and soul, wouldn't have been enough. She was saying, 'Stay with me,' and he'd say, 'Come with me.' She couldn't and he couldn't."[15]

David left.

Linda Gravenites had already told Myra Friedman that she couldn't adapt to the way Janis had changed. Janis didn't stop, and early in April, when Janis told Gravenites she either had to change her attitude or leave, Gravenites left.

Now all Janis had left was her career—which was about to enter its last stage.

Chapter 8

Full-Tilt Boogie to the End

Janis claimed that Linda Gravenites's departure shocked her so much she immediately quit heroin. Her new roommate, Lyndall Erb, who moved in with Janis the second week of April, agreed. For several weeks, it looked like she'd finally quit the drug completely, much to the relief of her friends.

On April 4, 1970, Janis performed in a reunion concert with Big Brother. Through the rest of the month she worked on creating a new band, this time with much more confidence than she'd had when the Kozmic Blues Band had been formed. She did away with the idea of a horn section and focused on the basics: guitar, John Till; bass, Brad Campbell (both carried over from the Kozmic Blues Band); piano, Richard Bell; organ, Ken Pearson; and drums, Clark Pierson.

Unlike the Kozmic Blues Band, the new band gelled right away. "These guys were looking for a band that was their home," John Cooke said. "They knew that Janis was the boss, and they all liked each other right away. I think the fact that four out of five were Canadian helped." As for Janis, he said, "Janis needed to love the people she worked with."[1]

Janis's new-found confidence as a band leader may be attributed to her achievement in finally having gotten off heroin. But getting off one drug just meant she used more of her other drug, the one that had always been her favorite: alcohol.

Pearl

Sometime during rehearsals with the new band, Janis decided, in discussions with various people, to craft a stage persona, a kind of mask to protect her "intimate self" from the public. The band members came up with the nickname Pearl for Janis one day, and Janis decided to adopt that name for her new persona.

"Pearl was way over the top, an often grotesque self-caricature," wrote Alice Echols. "Her closest friends cringed when she trotted out Pearl with feathers in her hair, not to mention all those boas." But, increasingly, the Pearl persona was the real Janis, at least the one most people saw. "There was a new hardness about her now, solidified by her eternal loneliness, the suspicion that everyone was out to use her, and not least, her twenty-four-hour boozing," wrote Echols.

Her loneliness was so great, even when Janis was at home and her house was crowded with people, she still felt alone.

Her house was crowded with people she barely knew. Janis didn't know who were her real friends. She felt that the only reason most of the people around her spent any time with her was because she was rich and famous and generous with drugs and booze. And the sad thing was, she was probably right.

Always desperate to be loved, Janis had scaled the heights of stardom only to find that she still couldn't be certain that anyone really loved her for herself.

The Great Tequila Boogie

As the debut of what had been dubbed the Full-Tilt Boogie Band in May grew closer, Janis's insecurities about her new musical direction once again came to the fore. Janis's friend Bobby Neuwirth, Bob Dylan's former road manager, and his friend, singer/songwriter Kris Kristofferson, then new on the scene, came to the rescue with something that became known as The Great Tequila Boogie.

Neuwirth and Kristofferson left a party in New York for California one night, and at four the next morning called Janis. Janis liked Kristofferson, and the party Neuwirth and Kristofferson had already begun became a three-week bash, with unending consumption of alcohol and an endless series of parties, culminating with one at Janis's house.

And then it was time for the debut of the group. Janis wanted her old road manager John Cooke back, and Cooke, who had quit because of her heroin use (he had no problem at all with her alcohol use) finally agreed to come when Bobby Neuwirth, an old friend of his, kept telling him how great Janis had been doing.

The debut was a private party being held by the Hell's Angels in San Rafael, California. Big Brother opened. There was almost a brawl as Janis's band went on stage when Janis refused to share some of her liquor with a biker. The next day, Janis told Myra Friedman she couldn't even remember how she'd sung or how the band had played, because she'd been drinking so much that she passed out after the concert. "I don't know what's happening to me!" she said.[2]

But the tour proper got off to a good start. The band was the best she'd ever had, and Janis was beginning to find new and more sophisticated ways to use her voice instead of her trademark wailing and howling.

The first tour date was on May 29 in Gainesville, Florida. *Rolling Stone* liked the new sound. Full-Tilt,

Kristofferson, Janis, and "Bobby McGee"

In 2004, Kris Kristofferson reminisced about Janis and her version of his most famous song.

"We hung out together for a month or so," Kristofferson says, "but I never heard her sing it when she was alive. The first time I heard her version of it was right after she had died. I flew down to Los Angeles and met with all the people at the Landmark Hotel, where she had died.

"Paul Rothchild, the producer, asked me to come by the studio the next day, because he wanted to play me something, and he played me her version of it.

"It was very moving . . ."[3]

wrote David Dalton, had "the virtues of spontaneity and freshness without being amateurish," and provided a solid "wall of sound" that let Janis's singing be "more controlled and at the same time more inventive."[4]

She even began singing country music again. She'd performed Kris Kristofferson's "Me and Bobby McGee" back in December, but now she added it to her regular set. Country, blues, and Texas music were what she had grown up on, and "Me and Bobby McGee" was her first step back toward bringing some of that material into her act.

> "I don't know what's happening to me!"
> — Janis Joplin

The Festival Express

After five weeks of touring in the East, the band headed up to Canada for a five-day train trip, punctuated by three concerts, across the country. The "Festival Express" included Ian and Sylvia, Delaney and Bonnie, Buddy Guy, the Grateful Dead, the New Riders of the Purple Sage, and others. The performers partied all the way.

"It really was like a vacation," remembered John Cooke. "Other people were doing the driving and there was this beautiful scenery outside. It became very celebratory. And people, including myself, drank a good deal of the day instead of just the evening."[5]

From Canada, the band traveled to Hawaii. Full-Tilt got to relax there, but Janis hustled on over to Austin as a surprise guest at Kenneth Threadgill's birthday party on July 10. Eight thousand people attended, many people performed, and Janis sang two Kris Kristofferson tunes, "Me and Bobby McGee" and "Sunday Mornin' Comin' Down."

Then it was back on tour—focusing not just on performing but on planning for the next album, the first one with the Full-Tilt Boogie Band. Kozmic Blues had only reached number five on the charts and hadn't produced any hit singles. New women—women such as Bette Midler—were reaching for the crown of "leading lady of rock."

Janis needed a producer for the new album, one that would understand her music and wouldn't create a rift between her and her band as had happened with Kozmic Blues. She came up with Paul Rothchild, a friend of John Cooke's, who had once told her he liked her singing. Rothchild had produced all of The Doors' albums and the Paul Butterfield Blues Band. At Cooke's urging, he came along for the final few tour dates, from July 11 in San Diego to August 12 at Harvard.

Sometime that summer, Janis received an invitation to her tenth high-school reunion, to be held on August 15. On June 25, on *The Dick Cavett Show*, she talked about going to the reunion. "They laughed me out of class, out of town, and out of the state—so I'm going home," she said. The audience roared, but notes Laura Joplin, "She must have winced when she realized what she had said on network television. Port Arthur wasn't so backward that we didn't get that channel."[6]

116

She appeared again on Dick Cavett on August 3, drunk and slurring her speech.

On August 12, the Full-Tilt Boogie Band's tour wrapped up at Harvard Stadium. There had been a lot of trouble at music festivals that summer—ever since Woodstock, in fact. Janis told the audience, urging them not to run riot. Although the police were out in force, even forcing John Cooke and some of the band members back into their hotel when they tried to walk to their car to drive to a restaurant after the show, Janis's concert was the first held there that had not been followed by vandalism.

High-School Reunion

The next day, Janis flew to Texas for her high-school reunion. She took an entourage with her: John Cooke, Bobby Neuwirth, and her limo driver, John Fisher.

The reunion did not go well.

She convinced her sister, Laura, to go with her to the reunion committee meeting. In the car, Laura confronted her with some of the things she'd said about her. "Think about it, Janis. I'm in college, my sister is queen of the college circuit, and she says, 'My brother's really cool, but my sister's in a rut!' Thanks a lot!"

Laura wrote: "She just sat with her head bowed. Thoughts ran through my mind. Should I be surprised? Did she ever think how her actions might affect others? Not in my experience."[7]

At the committee meeting, Janis discovered her classmates hadn't been particularly pleased by the things

117

she had said about her high-school classmates to the national media either, and felt unjustly attacked by her. Even her best friend from high school, Karleen Bennett, had decided that if Janis wanted to see her, she would have to call. Janis didn't call (her mother had told her Karleen had moved to Houston), and so she and Janis never met.

Janis asked Laura if her parents were proud of her. Laura said yes, they were fairly "bursting with pride." She added, "But you don't make it easy on them, you know. Janis, you told the national press that they kicked you out of the house at age fourteen! That's not true! How can you say that?"[8]

The next day Janis made eggs Benedict for her entourage and her family for breakfast, but her parents left, saying they had a prior commitment to attend the wedding of a friend's daughter.

In the midst of all the stories Janis was telling at breakfast, Laura wrote: "I stopped her cold . . . and asked the obvious: 'But are you happy'?" Janis replied, "I'm on top of the world," but when Laura asked her again, ". . . but are you happy?. . . all she could do was mumble some sounds that meant she wasn't going to answer a dumb question like that."

She showed up for the afternoon and evening reunion events wearing what Laura called "San Francisco rock clothes," and when Laura pointed out it was a reunion, not a concert, and she should just be

A photo of Janis taken in 1970.

herself, Janis snapped, "Stay out of other people's business."[9]

The reunion news conference with Janis, captured on film, shows, wrote Alice Echols, "more clearly perhaps than any other document of Janis's life—how very thin her armor was, how close she felt to the hurt and scorn of her high school years. Back among her classmates,

Janis found her tough-girl carapace shattering within minutes."

Asked what she remembered most about the town, she started to say she didn't remember, then paused and said, "No comment." (It was a very rare moment when Janis Joplin had no comment.) Asked how she differed from her classmates, she snapped, "I don't know. Why don't you ask them?" She said she couldn't remember if she went to the football games, and that she felt "apart" from her classmates, and that she wasn't even asked to the prom, although she turned it into a joke. "It's enough to make you want to sing the blues."[10]

The reunion dinner went quietly enough. Sam Monroe, the master of ceremonies, listed everyone's accomplishments—everyone's except Janis's—and finished with, "Is there anything I've missed?"

"Janis Joplin," someone said.

"Oh, yes, and Janis Joplin." Some applause and whistles, and Janis was presented with a gag gift: a tire "for having come the greatest distance."

Neither Janis nor her entourage stayed for the dance. As soon as she left, people began talking about how crazy she had been—when, in fact, she hadn't.

At least, not by Janis Joplin standards.

Things went downhill after the reunion dinner. Janis and her entourage went to the Pelican Club to see Jerry Lee Lewis. On June 12, in Louisville, she'd tried to visit him backstage and he'd refused to talk to her. She approached him backstage in Port Arthur after the show, and she introduced Laura as her sister. "You wouldn't be bad-looking," Jerry Lee Lewis snarled at Laura, "if you weren't trying to look like your sister."

Janis hit him. Lewis hit her back. Janis's friends led her out of the room. As they walked out, she kept repeating, "How could he do that? How could he do that?"

The next morning, Dorothy and Seth Joplin were furious to find Bobby Neuwirth asleep in the car with the motor running and John Fisher asleep on the couch. "It created tension in the house," Laura wrote. Myra Friedman and Alice Echols say there was a particularly nasty argument between Mrs. Joplin and her daughter.

"Janis had come to get even with her hometown, but her big weekend—touted on national television—had brought a string of humiliations instead," wrote Echols.[11]

The Forty-eight-Hour Fiancé

Back in California, Janis rewrote her will, which had formerly left everything to Michael. However she felt about her trip to Port Arthur—and accounts varied depending on who she was talking to—her opinion of her family seems to have changed: She revised the document so that half her estate went to her parents and a quarter each to Michael and Laura.

According to Laura, Janis was trying to make things right, and have the kind of life she'd always wanted. She began a romance with Seth Morgan, a student at Berkeley. They'd met just before the Full-Tilt Boogie

121

Band went on tour; now, wrote Myra Friedman, "she was smitten. Perhaps a day and a half passed before she and Seth were exchanging vows of love. In less than forty-eight hours they had begun to speak of marriage."[12]

Seth had his own money; he was one of the descendants of J. P. Morgan, one of the richest men of the nineteenth century, and wasn't overwhelmed by either Janis's money or her lifestyle. He wasn't even a fan. He did like to be seen with Janis, out and about in her wildly painted Porsche, but Janis actually preferred to stay at home, drink a glass of wine, and watch TV.

Janis was trying to make things right, and have the kind of life she'd always wanted.

They made plans for a wedding at sea, and Janis even asked her attorney, Bob Gordon, to draw up a prenuptial agreement. She told him that Seth treated her better than anyone she'd ever met and made her feel "more like a woman" than any other man ever had.

The marriage, if it had occurred, would probably have been a disaster. Seth Morgan became a junkie who eventually went to jail for robbing women, served three years of a five-year sentence, wrote a novel in prison, and died in 1990, along with his girlfriend, in a motorcycle accident. Morgan had alcohol, cocaine, and Percodan in his blood. Just before the crash, witnesses saw his girlfriend pounding on his back, begging him to slow down.

A New Album

Through September, Janis stayed in Los Angeles while
Seth stayed at Larkspur. She was recording her new
album at Sunset Sound, an independent studio (she was
the first CBS act to use an independent studio) in a
converted garage. "She had the studio, the producer,
a band she loved, and good material," Laura Joplin
wrote. "Work was great."[13]

At one point, during a break in recording, Janis sang
a song she'd written in a bar with Bobby Neuwirth,
"Mercedes Benz." She'd never intended to put it on
the record, but it ended up on tape anyway.

Everything was going great, it seemed, but one day
in mid-September, her heroin-using friend and sometime
lover Peggy Caserta ended up at the Landmark Hotel in
Los Angeles where the band was staying. Janis didn't
know she was there. When she found out, she first
wanted Caserta to leave, but Janis ended up begging her
to share her heroin.

She told Seth Morgan she'd started using again
because "I couldn't get to work for being so. . . drunk
all the time. When the album's over I'll kick like
before."[14] She only shot up at night, after she finished
recording.

She told Peggy Caserta that Jimi Hendrix dying
lessened her chances of dying, because two such famous
rock stars couldn't go out in one year.

The Final Hours

On Saturday, October 3, 1970, Janis and the Full-Tilt
Boogie Band recorded the instrumental tracks for
"Buried Alive." Janis would come in and do the vocals
the next day.

Recording finished around 11 P.M. Janis stopped for
a drink at Barney's Beanery, then headed back to the
hotel, where she had two more drinks.

Sometime after returning to the hotel, she injected
herself with heroin, just pushing it under her skin
instead of directly into a vein. "Skin-popping," as that
technique was called, gave a delayed maximum impact,
of up to ninety minutes.

She'd bought the heroin at 4 P.M. from her usual
supplier, who went by the name of George. He usually
had a chemist check the heroin he sold before he sold it.
That night his chemist was out of town, so George sold
it without checking it. Later tests revealed that what she
had bought was four to ten times stronger than what
was normally sold on the street.

At 1 A.M., she showed up in the lobby to buy
cigarettes. The desk clerk gave her change for five
dollars.

Janis went back to her room. Sitting on the bed
wearing a blouse and panties, she put the cigarettes on
the bedside table. Still holding the change the desk clerk
had given her, she fell forward, striking her lip on the
bedside table.

Her body wasn't found until 7:30 P.M. the next day, wedged between the table and the bed. John Cooke said he discovered her. Seth Morgan had called him because he couldn't get hold of her, and Cooke had found out from Paul Rothchild that she was late for recording, which was very unusual for her.

Cooke sent someone to the airport to tell Morgan. After a doctor and the police had arrived, he drove to the studio and told Paul Rothchild and the band.

The coroner ruled that the death was due to an accidental overdose. Most likely it was because of the combined effects of alcohol and heroin in her system. Several other people died in Los Angeles of overdoses that same weekend. All had bought the extra-strong heroin from the same supplier.

Janis's friends were devastated. Dave Getz said he cried hysterically for hours. Many of them felt guilty. "Did we do this?" Kris Kristofferson is reported to have said as he looked at her body.

After they got the news, Janis's parents flew out to California to take care of Janis's affairs. There would be no funeral: Janis's will stipulated that her body be cremated. Her ashes were to be scattered off the California coast near Marin.

The Full-Tilt Boogie Band finished the album. Called *Pearl*, it's considered by many critics to be the best Janis Joplin album of all.

Chapter 9

The Aftermath and the Legacy

There are two sides to the legacy of Janis Joplin. On the one hand, she is a kind of shorthand for the dangers of drug abuse and the perils of rock stardom. (Jimi Hendrix fits that role as well.) On the other hand, she left a musical legacy that has resonated through rock for more than thirty years.

"When someone gets killed in an auto crash it doesn't make me stop driving," Grace Slick said. "Why print all that stuff about someone who's dead? She's gone, it's done."[1]

Bob Weir of the Grateful Dead said, "I can't bring myself to be in abject misery about it because, like I say, she drank herself to death, she lived up to her image."[2]

Dave Getz of Big Brother thought other musicians worried that the "whole place would have gone dead" if they'd really confronted what Janis's death meant. "Maybe it should have," he added.[3]

But Janis Joplin was also more than just a "tragic

victim," unlike the character strongly based on her played by Bette Midler in the 1979 movie *The Rose* (which was originally going to be titled *Pearl*). "The press seldom writes about her fun-loving character, her concentration on art, or her social attitudes, which were so familiar to those of us who knew her," noted Laura Joplin.[4]

On January 19, 1988, on what would have been Janis Joplin's forty-fifth birthday, Port Arthur dedicated a museum exhibit honoring Janis and a bronze statue in her honor. More than five thousand people attended. The exhibit included all kinds of memorabilia from Janis's early life, handpicked by her mother, Dorothy.

Accompanying it, because many Port Arthur citizens didn't want to honor Janis, were other exhibits about other famous musicians from the area: Johnny and Edgar Winter, the Big Bopper, Tex Ritter, ZZ Top, George Jones, and others. But Janis was the chief honoree.

Janis's House Becomes a Rehab Center

In 1999, a house where Janis lived in the Haight-Ashbury district in 1967 and 1968 was turned into a drug rehabilitation center.

"I think Janis would be really pleased and happy to have this happen," said Country Joe McDonald, Janis's one-time lover. "She'd like to know something good was being done with that house."

Ironically, however, music was not allowed in the house, because it would distract people trying to live together and quit drugs.[5]

Joplin's musical legacy is still felt today. Melissa Etheridge (left) and Joss Stone performed "Cry Baby/Piece of My Heart" in a tribute to Janis at the 47th Annual Grammy Awards in 2005.

Her musical legacy is best summed up by comments from today's musicians who look to Janis Joplin as an inspiration:

Stevie Nicks said, "I only saw Janis Joplin one time—on a hot summer day in San Jose, California . . . She was extraordinary. She had a connection with the audience that I had not seen before, and when she left the stage—I knew that a little bit of my destiny had changed—I would search to find that connection that I had seen between Janis and her audience. In a blink of an eye—she changed my life."

> **"I would search to find that connection that I had seen between Janis and her audience. In a blink of an eye—she changed my life."**
> **—Stevie Nicks**

Joan Jett: "When I first heard the primal scream in 'Piece of My Heart,' I was hooked . . . I couldn't help but go to the mirror and pretend I was a wild woman like Janis, in a rock band."

Etta James: "Janis was like an angel who came and paved a road white chicks hadn't walked before."

Pink: "I have a deep, spiritual connection to Janis. And I don't know how, why or when. But, I've always been extremely attracted to her energy, and her pain, and her voice, and her life. I just think she is one of the most amazing women that ever lived." [6]

There's a tendency, Alice Echols notes, for people to think of Janis as just the same as the "nineties riot grrrls" and "slickly packaged agro-rock" of recent years. What they miss is that Janis, vulnerable, ambitious, needy, in pain, always seeking reassurance (and she was all of those, often all at once), had no role models of her own when she moved out to San Francisco and decided to be a rock singer.

She was a true American rebel.

1943 **January 19:** Janis Lyn Joplin is born at 9:30 A.M. to Seth and Dorothy Joplin at St. Mary's Hospital, Port Arthur, Texas.

1958 Reads about Jack Kerouac and the Beats in *Time* magazine.

1960 **May:** Graduates from Thomas Jefferson High School in Port Arthur.

Fall: Attends Lamar State College of Technology in Beaumont.

1961 **March:** Enrolls in business college in Port Arthur.

Summer: Passes secretarial exam, moves to Los Angeles, works as a keypunch operator.

Fall: Moves to North Beach, San Francisco, mingles with local beatniks.

Christmas: Returns to Port Arthur; New Year's Eve performs at bar in Beaumont but is cut off after one number.

1962 **Winter:** Makes first recording, a jingle: "This Bank Is Your Bank." Attends classes at Lamar State College of Technology.

Summer: Enrolls at the University of Texas.

Fall: Attends classes at the University of Texas. Nominated for "Ugliest Man on Campus." Sings with local bluegrass band, the Waller Creek Boys. Performs at Threadgill's.

1963 **January 23:** Arrives in San Francisco with Chet Helms.

Winter and Spring: Sings in coffeehouses. Meets Peter Albin and James Gurley, future members of Big Brother and the Holding Company.

Summer and Fall: Supposed to perform at upcoming San Francisco State Music Festival but never shows. Hurts leg in a motorcycle accident. Gets arrested for shoplifting.

1964 **Summer:** Moves to New York.

Fall: Returns to San Francisco. Performs regularly at coffeehouses. Realizes she's addicted to speed.

1965 **Winter and Spring:** Begins using heroin. Meets Peter de Blanc; becomes engaged. She decides to give up drugs and returns to Port Arthur to prepare for the wedding.

May: Registers for classes at Lamar Tech.

August: Peter de Blanc visits. Janis's father gives him permission to marry Janis.

November: She sings at the Half-Way House in Beaumont; gets a rave review in Austin paper.

Christmas: Realizes wedding is never going to happen.

1966 **Winter and Spring:** Continues classes at Lamar Tech; also sings in Austin clubs.

March: Sings at benefit for Texas blues singer Teodar Jackson.

May: In San Francisco, Big Brother and the Holding Company is looking for a "chick singer"; Chet Helms suggests Janis.

June 4: Arrives in San Francisco and auditions for Big Brother.

June 10: Performs with Big Brother for the first time.

July 1: Moves to a house in Lagunitas with members of Big Brother, their wives, and girlfriends.

August 23: Big Brother begins a four-week engagement in Chicago that doesn't go well.

September: Out of money and stranded, Big Brother signs a deal with Mainstream Records

Fall: Big Brother records, first in Chicago, then in Los Angeles. First single, "Blindman," is released, goes nowhere.

1967   **January 4:** The Human Be-In in Golden Gate Park.

June 17: First performance of Big Brother at Monterey Pop Festival.

June 18: A second performance of Big Brother added Sunday night so they can be filmed.

November: Big Brother hires Albert Grossman as manager.

1968   **February 16:** First New York appearance by Janis and Big Brother garners rave reviews and launches East Coast tour.

March–April: *Cheap Thrills* album recording sessions in New York and Hollywood, billing of band changed to feature Janis Joplin.

August: *Cheap Thrills* album released, sells more than a million copies in the first month.

September: Announcement that Janis and Big Brother are parting ways. Tensions in the group caused by the split sometimes spill over on stage.

November: Mike Bloomfield and Nick Gravenites agree to help Janis form a new band.

November 15: Last East Coast performance with Big Brother.

December 1: Big Brother's last performance with Janis Joplin, in San Francisco.

December 18–19: New band assembled and rehearsed; called the Kozmic Blues Band.

December 21: New band makes debut at the Stax/Volt "Yuletide Thing" in Memphis; gets cool reception.

1969   **February 11–12:** Band kicks off tour at Fillmore East, to mixed reaction.

March 4: CBS's *60 Minutes* documentary "Carnegie Hall for Children" includes backstage footage of Janis.

March 15: Damaging interview with Janis in *Rolling Stone* titled "Janis: The Judy Garland of Rock?"

March 18: Janis sings on *The Ed Sullivan Show*.

April–May: Makes a well-received European tour.

June: Recording sessions for the *Kozmic Blues* album begin in Hollywood.

July 18: Janis makes first appearance on *The Dick Cavett Show*.

August 16: Janis and the band perform at Woodstock, not a great performance.

August 31: Performance better received at International Pop Festival in Lewisville, Texas.

November: *Kozmic Blues* album released; Janis charged with two counts of using vulgar and obscene language in Tampa.

December: Moves into new house in Larkspur, California.

1970   **January:** Kozmic Blues Band disbanded.

February–March: Flies to Brazil for Carnival, gets clean of heroin. Meets David Niehaus; plan to return to San Francisco together, but he has visa problems. By the time he arrives, Janis is back on heroin; Niehaus leaves soon after.

April: Assembles final band, Full-Tilt Boogie.

April 4: Sings in reunion concert with Big Brother at the Fillmore West.

May: Full-Tilt plays first gig, a Hell's Angels dance, then launches tour in Florida.

June 25: Janis on *The Dick Cavett Show* for the second time.

June 28–July 4: "Festival Express" tour across Canada.

July 10: Sings at birthday celebration for Ken Threadgill in Austin.

August 3: Last appearance on *The Dick Cavett Show.*

August 12: Last live performance, at Harvard Stadium.

August 14: Attends high-school reunion in Port Arthur, Texas.

September: *Pearl* recording sessions in Los Angeles.

October 4: 1:40 A.M. Janis dies alone in her hotel room of a heroin overdose, combined with alcohol.

Discography

Janis Joplin recorded two albums with Big Brother and the Holding Company, one with the Kozmic Blues Band, and one with the Full-Tilt Boogie Band. Since her death, a number of compilations and remastered recordings have also been released. This discography includes only the albums produced during her life (or, in the case of the final album, shortly after her death).

Big Brother and the Holding Company

Big Brother and the Holding Company, Mainstream Records, 1968

By, Bye Baby
Easy Rider
Intruder
Light Is Faster Than Sound
Call on Me
Women Is Losers
Blindman
Down on Me
Caterpillar
All Is Loneliness

Cheap Thrills, Columbia, 1968

Combination of the Two
I Need a Man to Love

Summertime
Piece of My Heart
Turtle Blues
Oh, Sweet Mary
Ball and Chain

Kozmic Blues Band

I Got Dem Ol' Kozmic Blues Again, Mama! Columbia, 1969

Try (Just a Little Bit Harder)
Maybe
One Good Man
As Good as You've Been to This World
To Love Somebody
Kozmic Blues
Little Girl Blue
Work Me, Lord

Full-Tilt Boogie Band

Pearl, Columbia, 1971

Move Over
Cry Baby
A Woman Left Lonely
Half Moon
Buried Alive in the Blues
My Baby
Me and Bobby McGee
Mercedes Benz
Trust Me
Get It While You Can

Further Reading

Books

Balcavage, Dynise. *Janis Joplin*. Philadelphia, Pa.: Chelsea House, 2001.

Joplin, Laura. *Love, Janis*. New York: HarperCollins, 2005.

Maga, Timothy; foreword by Donald A. Ritchie. *The 1960s*. New York, NY: Facts On File, Inc., 2003.

Matthews, Glenna. *American Women's History: A Student Companion*. New York: Oxford University Press, 2000.

Woog, Adam. *Rock and Roll Legends*. San Diego, CA: Lucent Books, 2001.

Internet Addresses

The Official Janis Joplin Site
  <http://www.officialjanis.com/>

Janisjoplin.net
  <http://www.janisjoplin.net/>

The Rock and Roll Hall of Fame and Museum
  <http://www.rockhall.com/inductee/janis-joplin>

Chapter Notes

Introduction

1. Echols, Alice, *Scars of Sweet Paradise: The Life and Times of Janis Joplin*, New York: Metropolitan Books, 1999, p. 165.
2. Joplin, Laura, *Love, Janis*, New York: HarperCollins 2005, p. 237.

Chapter 1. Frilled Frocks and Bridge

1. Storey, John W., "Port Arthur, Texas," The Handbook of Texas Online, <http://www.tsha. utexas.edu/handbook/online/articles/PP/ hdp5.html> (September 22, 2006).
2. Joplin, Laura, *Love, Janis*, New York: Penguin Books, 1992 p. 25.
3. Ibid., p. 25
4. Ibid., p. 27.
5. Friedman, Myra, *Buried Alive: The Biography of Janis Joplin*, New York: Harmony Books, 1992, p. 10.
6. Ibid., p. 13.

Chapter 2. The Rebellion Begins

1. Friedman, Myra, *Buried Alive: The Biography of Janis Joplin*, New York: Harmony Books, 1992, p. 12.
2. Ibid., p. 14.
3. Joplin, Laura, *Love, Janis*, New York: Penguin Books, 1992 pp. 43.

4. Echols, Alice, *Scars of Sweet Paradise: The Life and Times of Janis Joplin*, New York: Metropolitan Books, 1999 p. 12.

5. Joplin, p. 48.

6. Ibid., p. 44–45.

7. Ibid., p. 46.

8. "The Beat Generation and the Birth of Counter-Culture," *Weekend Edition*, National Public Radio, May 22, 1994.

9. Echols, p. 21.

10. Ibid., p. 22.

11. Joplin, p. 68.

12. Ibid., p. 71.

Chapter 3. From College to the Coast

1. Echols, Alice, *Scars of Sweet Paradise: The Life and Times of Janis Joplin*, New York: Metropolitan Books, 1999 p. 27.

2. Ibid., p. 28.

3. Echols, p. 37.

4. Hansen, Liane (host), "Profile: Impact of Kenneth Threadgill and his club, Threadgill's, on the Austin music sccnc," Weekend Edition – Sunday (NPR), September 21, 2003.

5. Ibid., pp. 124–126.

6. Echols, p. 44.

7. Joplin, Laura, *Love Janis,* New York: Penguin Books, 1992, p. 137.

8. Gilmore, John. "Celebrity Spotlight – Janis Joplin." <http://www.johngilmore.com/Celebrities/janisjoplin.html> (September 21, 2006).

Chapter 4. New York to L.A.

1. Joplin, Laura, *Love, Janis*, New York: Harper Books, 2005, p. 140.
2. Echols, Alice, *Scars of Sweet Paradise: The Life and Times of Janis Joplin*, New York: Metropolitan Books, 1999, p. 82.
3. Joplin, p. 143.
4. Joplin, p. 146.
5. Friedman, Myra, *Buried Alive: The Biography of Janis Joplin*, New York: Harmony Books 1992, p. 57.
6. Joplin, p. 152.
7. Ibid., p. 154.
8. Echols, p. 112.
9. Ibid., p. 114.
10. Joplin, p. 176.
11. Ibid., p. 174.

Chapter 5. Haight-Ashbury

1. Echols, Alice, *Scars of Sweet Paradise: The Life and Times of Janis Joplin*, New York: Metropolitan Books, 1999, p. 127.
2. Kippel, Les and Bromberg, Robert. "Big Brother Speaks: An Interview With Peter Albin," Relix, October 1, 1992. <http://www.janisjoplin.net/articles/Janis.php?page=23> (September 18, 2006).
3. "Comments from Janis," Hit Parader, September 1, 1970. <http://www.janisjoplin.net/articles/Janis.php?page=39> (September 18, 2006).
4. Joplin, Laura, *Love, Janis*, New York: Harper Books 2005, p. 188.

5. Friedman, Myra, *Buried Alive: The Biography of Janis Joplin*, New York: Harmony Books 1992, p. 76.

6. Joplin, p. 194.

7. Echols, p. 197.

8. Ibid., p. 150.

9. Ibid., p. 157.

10. Joplin, p. 229.

Chapter 6. To Monterey and Beyond!

1. Echols, Alice, *Scars of Sweet Paradise: The Life and Times of Janis Joplin*, New York: Metropolitan Books 1999, p. 165.

2. Joplin, Laura, *Love, Janis*, New York: Harper Books, 2005, p. 236.

3. Joplin, pp. 245–246.

4. Ibid., pp. 250–251.

5. Echols, p. 178.

6. Ibid., pp. 181–182.

7. Ibid., p. 196.

8. Friedman, Myra, *Buried Alive: The Biography of Janis Joplin*, New York: Harmony Books 1992, p. 114.

9. Echols, p. 205.

10. Friedman, p. 119.

11. Joplin, p. 277.

12. Ibid., p. 278.

Chapter 7. Kozmic Blues

1. Echols, Alice, *Scars of Sweet Paradise: The Life and Times of Janis Joplin*, New York: Metropolitan Books, 1999, p.229.
2. Friedman, Myra, *Buried Alive: The Biography of Janis Joplin*, New York: Harmony Books, 1992, p. 145.
3. Nelson, Paul. "Janis: The Judy Garland of Rock?" Rolling Stone, March 15, 1969. <http://www.janisjoplin.net/articles/janis.php?page=46>, (September 18, 2006).
4. Friedman, p. 148.
5. Echols, p. 244.
6. Ibid., p. 247.
7. Freidman, p. 161.
8. Ibid., p. 266.
9. Joplin, p. 309.
10. Friedman, p. 174.
11. Echols, p. 268.
12. Friedman, p. 178.
13. Joplin, p. 318.
14. Echols, p. 272.
15. Friedman, p. 190.

Chapter 8. Full-Tilt Boogie to the End

1. Joplin, Laura, *Love, Janis*, New York: Harper Books 2005, p. 331.
2. Friedman, Myra, *Buried Alive: The Biography of Janis Joplin*, New York: Harmony Books 1992, p. 201.

3. Pendreigh, Brian. "Kristofferson opens up at last about the real Bobby McGee; Singer talks about life with Janis Joplin and the death of Johnny Cash." *The Mail on Sunday*, February 8, 2004.

4. Echols, Alice, *Scars of Sweet Paradise: The Life and Times of Janis Joplin*, New York: Metropolitan Books, 1999., p. 280.

5. Joplin, p. 344.

6. Ibid., p. 355.

7. Ibid., p. 357.

8. Ibid., p. 359.

9. Ibid., p. 360.

10. Ibid., pp. 363–364.

11. Echols, p. 291.

12. Friedman, p. 292.

13. Joplin, p. 368.

14. Ibid., p. 369.

Chapter 9. The Aftermath and the Legacy

1. Echols, Alice, *Scars of Sweet Paradise: The Life and Times of Janis Joplin*, New York: Metropolitan Books, 1999, p. 303.

2. Ibid.

3. Ibid.

4. Joplin, Laura, *Love, Janis*, New York: Harper Books 2005, p. 379.

5. "New Role for Joplin house," *The Birmingham Post*, May 22, 1999.

6. "Reflections," janisjoplin.net, <http://www.janisjoplin.net/reflections/> (September 18, 2006).

Glossary

beatnik—Name given to people who did not conform in dress and behavior to society's rules in the 1950s.

Billboard—A magazine devoted to the music industry.

bluegrass—A type of folk music that originated in the southern United States, typically played on banjos and guitars and characterized by rapid tempos and jazz-like improvisation.

blues—A kind of jazz that evolved from the music of African-Americans, especially work songs and spirituals, in the early twentieth century. Blues pieces often express worry or depression.

cover—A new version of a previously recorded song.

folk music—A type of music created by the regular people of a region and passed down from person to person, instead of on paper. Some "folk" music is composed by people who are inspired by real folk music and imitate its sound.

gold record—Awarded to an artist or group whose album has sold more than 500,000 copies or a single, one song, has sold over one million copies.

heroin—A dangerous and addictive drug, illegal in the United States and many other countries. It is derived from the opium poppy plant.

hippies—People in the 1960s and 1970s who rejected many standard American traditions and social and political ideas.

homosexual—Someone who has intimate relationships with a person of the same gender.

hootenanny—An informal concert or gathering where folk singers would perform; usually with audience participation.

integration—Bringing people of different races or ethnic to equality.

LSD—An illegal and addictive drug. The drug, lysergic acid diethylamide, causes hallucinations.

marijuana—A drug that causes hallucinations. It is illegal to grow or possess in the United States.

overdose—The ingestion of too much of a substance, generally some type of drug.

royalty—A share of the profits made from a recording or other piece of work.

segregation—Separating people at schools, neighborhoods, jobs and public properties based on race, gender, social class, or ethnicity.

speed—a stimulant, such as amphetamine or methamphetamine. It is illegal and addictive.

Index